RIDDING YOURSELF
OF UNHAPPINESS

First Published 1985
by The Barry Long Foundation
BCM Box 876 London WC1N 3XX

Reprinted 1987, 1989

ISBN 0 9508050 2 5

Set in 12 on 14pt Century Book by Grassroots Typeset
and printed and bound in Great Britain by
Biddles Ltd, Guildford and King's Lynn

Part of this text, pages 149–190,
was recorded on cassette by
The Barry Long Foundation in
April 1985. It is available as
'The Law of Life (Karma)', the
sixth of Barry Long's
Myth of Life tapes.

Also by Barry Long:
Meditation—A Foundation Course
Knowing Yourself
The Origins of Man and the Universe
The Myth of Life (Cassette Series)
Stillness Is The Way

RIDDING YOURSELF
OF UNHAPPINESS

BARRY LONG

You have opened this book because unhappiness is in you.

You may not be unhappy at this moment. But you will be tomorrow or the next day. Happy today, unhappy tomorrow — that's normal. And that *is* unhappiness.

You long to be free of that uncertainty and this book is to help you.

It is not an ordinary book.

It is energetic, spiritually energetic.

That means it is true to what it says it is. It does the job. Whether you believe it or not is of no consequence. It works direct, immediately, now, in your subconscious where all unhappiness is lodged.

Nothing in the book has to be remembered. What is energetic — and only the spirit is energetic — does not have to be remembered: it reminds you.

Unhappiness is ignorance.

You cannot *be* happy: to think that or want it is ignorance because whatever you aim for or achieve cannot last — and then you will be unhappy again. You can only be free of unhappiness. That alone lasts. When you are free of unhappiness, what is there to want?

Ignorance is the accumulation of all the past emotional hurt and pain you are pleased to ignore in yourself because you feel it is too painful to face.

Why face it when you can run from it?

The trouble is that when you run from ignorance or emotional pain in yourself you run from life — and sooner or later you start to feel dead, don't you?

So this live, energetic book is going to point up your unhappiness while bringing you to life.

Now, this is how the book works.

There is no unhappiness in the book itself. The book and I do not care whether you read it or not, whether you like it or not, or whether you agree with what is in it or not. Whatever way it affects you will not make the book or I unhappy.

Any unhappiness or disturbance is in you alone.

The more intensely anything in the book upsets or disturbs you, it is a signal that that particular association is a deep hidden source of unhappiness in you.

It means you are holding on to something that makes you unhappy, something it pleases you to think is in the book when it is in you. You have something to defend in you, something you are choosing to go on hiding from yourself. So you defend it with your judgement of the book or myself, instead of looking at why it pains you and why you need to defend it or justify it at all.

You cannot judge anything in this book.

If you do, it will be your unhappiness judging.

To use the book you must read it over and over for the rest of your life — or until all unhappy reactions in you have vanished. How to deal energetically with reactions is described in the first section.

What is in you is also outside you.

So the book is going to highlight areas in your daily life where you are in fact deeply unhappy and which you are doing nothing about because you are happy to fool yourself that there is nothing really wrong.

You won't like that. And if you are quick you will see that that is the point. What you don't like is what you are unhappy about — and not facing up to.

Anything you are moved to criticise in what you read will be an energetic reflection of something in your work, love, partnership or family life that you are unhappy about and avoiding: you are choosing to find the problem in the book where it is not, instead of in your life where it is.

The book is for you. Read it.

And make the blessed earth that much happier where you are.

Barry Long

Section One

DYING TO YOURSELF

Section Two

THE HARDEST DEATH
part one
DYING TO THE WORLD
part two
DYING TO EXISTENCE

Section Three

THE LAW OF LIFE (KARMA)
part one
DYING FOR LIFE
part two
DYING TO BE BORN

Guide to contents

Only fear dies

Section One

DYING TO YOURSELF

1
THE UNHAPPY UNHAPPY-BODY

Unhappiness is substantial. It lives in you.

At this moment, even though you may be tranquil or untroubled, unhappiness is there. Periodically and inevitably it will rise up and you will be unhappy — depressed, self-doubting, self-pitying, lonely, resentful or sad — without knowing why.

Unhappiness is not natural in you. It has invaded you from the external world since your conception in the womb.

The invasion started through the medium of similarly acquired unhappiness residing in your mother's body. And since infancy, due to the ignorance of your parents, associates, teachers and then yourself of the cause of unhappiness, unhappiness has been allowed to continue to enter you and grow in you.

It is now a sturdy, health-eroding, degenerative living body the same age as yourself.

The substance of your unhappy-body is your emotions.

You may think you get pleasure out of your emotions. But it's a fickle pleasure — an emotional high — that never lasts because its opposite pole is a fickle pain, an emotional low. The two are a see-saw. You can't have one without the other.

Emotional pleasure arises from the stimulus of excitement. Then, as the excitement dies the pleasure disappears. And you gradually become bored, restless, confused or unhappy — until another stimulus comes along.

You are up for a while, then down. That is your life. Up and down. Pleasure precedes pain, pain precedes pleasure. And in between, preventing you from connecting the two up and seeing the truth of how your life is being manipulated, is the dreaded emptiness of boredom and aloneness.

Aloneness, like boredom, is intolerable to the emotions. It is felt as acute loneliness or isolation. To the emotions, aloneness and boredom are like death, the end of any hope of stimulus or excitement.

So, to avoid this dreaded state, and if no stimulating or exciting pleasurable activity is around to look forward to, the emotions revive in you the *stimulus* of past unhappy feelings. You are then depressed or "down" without knowing why.

In time, as your unhappy-body develops, you begin subconsciously to enjoy the see-sawing stimulus itself — the downs as well as the ups. Whether the emotions are pleasurable or painful is no longer that important. As long as they are stimulated or active — a high or low — you feel emotionally alive, which is felt to

2

be far preferable to feeling emotionally "dead" or alone.

Finally, by the time your unhappy-body matures, you are emotionally hooked.

You are then addicted to the perverse pleasure of emotional pain or unhappiness. You cling to it — as your moods and depressions. You enjoy it.

When you are next moody or depressed — will you give it up, now? No. You will say you can't or you won't. You enjoy your unhappiness too much to let go of it.

The fact that it's painful and that you protest at the time how unhappy you are, is irrelevant. The truth is you prefer this pain you know to the simple pain you refuse to face — the pain of being alone without stimulus. When you start to face it, the pain eventually becomes the never-ending joy or bliss of being or feeling yourself.

This unhappy living substance which you mistakenly think is you, is your emotional body.

Your unhappy emotional body, however, does not have it all its own way. It is continuously being undermined by your natural happy self.

In fact, in the loving and spiritual moments of your life the unhappy-body is actually being reduced. But through avoidance of the cause of unhappiness in the rest of your daily living the unhappiness destroyed is more or less replaced.

The result is that you are forced to share your life with your unhappy moods and depressions. When you, your happy self, are buoyant, the unhappy-body is dormant. When the unhappy-body is buoyant, you are dormant. Each of you has your days in the one physical body.

3

It is a very strange way of life. As everyone is living it, or doing it, it is said to be normal, which is true. But it is not natural.

What is natural is not normal. The natural state of man and woman is joy within. You are joy — beneath your normal to-and-froing emotions.

And unlike anything that is normal, natural joy or bliss within has no opposite.

2
THE PART OR PURITY OF SEX

All the unhappy moments of your life live on in you now as your unhappy emotional body.

Every single hurt of childhood — the times you sobbed in your locked room, lost your closest friend, were bullied at school, pined and fretted out of loneliness and injustice — is still there. All those unhappy, unconsoled children or emotions weep on in you, the adult of the little boy or little girl you were.

Those earliest of emotions did not remain fragmented. In their pain and isolation they drew together inside you. Building up one on top of the other in living layers of feeling, they compressed themselves into a sad and lonely emotional ball. This is centred in your stomach area.

In childhood this small, moody, unhappy ball had little strength or force. You were able to be easily distracted from it and to throw off your gloomy self pretty quickly.

But with puberty this changed.

For the natural, happy physical body, the inflowing sexual or reproductive energy marked the arrival of pure sensual wisdom or power — and under its deep enriching influence your body matured beautifully and naturally throughout the puberty period.

Moreover, the new energy gradually imparted to your happy body the natural or divine ability to create more natural happiness or joy in other bodies; that is, in the bodies of the happy mates it would be capable of making love with perfectly and instinctively; and in the new happy physical baby bodies that would be naturally formed and born out of those unions.

It was — and still is if you want it — a supremely beautiful and yet thoroughly practical design for life or love on earth.

Combined with the self-consciousness that only man and woman possess of all the species, the result was to be a continuous expansion in the flesh of the joy and wonder of consciously participating in life on this planet.

But the presence of the unhappy unhappy-body ruined it — for you and everyone.

In nature, no unhappiness or emotion exists in its own right. No provision is made for its survival or evolution in any organ or organism, including the human body. It is completely parasitic and destructive of the good and the right — the natural.

Consequently, the unhappy-body's unnatural existence in the physical at the climacteric age of puberty, created an enormous distortion and distraction in the natural perception of the senses. The incredible extent of this distortion and distraction is before you now as your pain-and-pleasure existence — the world of problems and ill-health — which everyone correctly regards as normal, and erroneously regards as natural and unavoidable.

At puberty, the new incoming sexual energy, while greatly strengthening your happy physical body, also necessarily strengthened the parasitic unhappy-body.

But while the physical was able to adapt perfectly to the transforming potency of the energy and reach the full power of sexual maturity and sexual wisdom, the young unhappy-body was utterly incapable of accommodating it or coping with it.

Being without wisdom or maturity — because these qualities emerge only from inner joy — the young unhappy emotional body could not receive the generative power of the energy. It could only react as a resistance. The effect of that was that in pushing its way through the unhappy-body the energy's purity and power degenerated into the impurity of force.

Force is neither power nor strength. Force is the beginning of violence and all violence begins in the unhappy and insecure emotional bodies of men and women.

The first appearance of this unhappy degenerative force in the world is the normal headstrong ignorance and wilful independence of adolescence expressing itself as a more or less blind determination to find pleasure or love through excitement — and not in oneself.

At the same time, another remarkable thing was

happening. This also was determining normal adolescent and subsequent adult behaviour.

The pure sex energy of puberty immediately began destroying the unhappy emotional body or growth and purging the unhappy effects, the force, from the body.

The expulsion of this force manifested externally in adolescence as an almost constant psychic or nervous discontent — a wanting to be always mentally, emotionally or physically engaged in some activity, without necessarily doing anything but wanting it. This same restlessness, mellowed by the weight of experience, continues in you the adult today, making it virtually impossible for you to remain free of thoughts, or at peace with yourself, for any length of time without the aid of some external stimulus.

After puberty, you also could no longer be so easily distracted from the pull of your emotions. Their hold was stronger. And unsuspectingly you were attaching yourself to them, by amusing and gratifying yourself with the new stimulating pleasure of sexual or romantic fantasising.

By indulging in any kind of erotic imagining you were playing with the full force of unhappiness. But of course in your ignorance you did not know it — any more than you know it today if you continue to do this. All that mattered to the adolescent, immature unhappy-body, was that the incoming sexual energy offered the ultimate in excitement — a fantastic new means of selfish pleasure. The fact that there were strings attached — that there is no such thing as a free lunch — never occurred to you.

Underneath all the imaginings and the turbulent

emotions the images provoked, the inflowing stream of pure sex energy was absolutely constant and unvarying in its richness and fullness. But felt through the resistance of the unhappy emotional body the energy appeared to be intermittent — rising as sexual urges or excitement which, while they lasted, produced an incomparably intense and pleasurable emotional high.

But — and now I must talk to you, the adult, in your present experience — as soon as the sexual stimulus or cause of it ends, the excited emotional body starts to slow down. It slows down until once again you feel calm or normal.

However, no "normal" or constant feeling is possible in the emotional body. It is never stable. It is either going up or going down — and much of the feeling of this occurs beneath your awareness.

So, after being excited and then seeming to calm down, the unhappy-body actually keeps on calming or slowing down until sooner or later — within hours or days — its vibration-pitch reaches the dreaded in-between rate felt as boredom, isolation or aloneness.

To get out of this, and in an attempt to regain the lost pleasure or stimulus of the high, the emotional body forces you to think about past exciting experiences — usually sexual.

This makes it vibrate at the intensity of a high and the feeling is very pleasant. How often have you done this lying in bed or in a hot bath?

But as soon as the imaginative stimulus ends, that is, when you stop thinking, or turn your attention elsewhere, the emotional body continues to vibrate on its own. And since it is a negative unhappy organism it cannot help but create in itself the opposite unhappy effect — an equally intense low or depression. This, hours or days after, surfaces in your awareness as a nasty, gloomy feeling of lack or emptiness — you are then depressed or moody without knowing why. Soon it turns into a desire or craving to repeat the pleasure now painfully felt to be missing.

This craving then drives you to engage in external activity to try to repeat the pleasure of the high.

The activity is usually sexual, or a normal self-gratifying substitute such as appeasing an appetite for food, spending, alcohol, clothes, entertaining, money — in short, some sort of passing pleasure. Inevitably, this leads to more discontent and unhappiness; and this in turn to more craving, more misguided action, more pain and so on.

The cycle of pleasure and pain continues uninterrupted for the entire life or until a conscious stand is made to dissolve the unhappy-body — and be yourself.

Meanwhile, through your emotions — not only the residual ball but through the new pains arriving thick and fast as a result of fresh sexual experiences and pressures — you learn to fear what caused them, and how to erect emotional barriers to prevent the same pains hurting you again.

These self-protective devices then grow into emotional calluses.

The emotional calluses insulate but dull your feelings — and so gradually you feel more and more dead. The enjoyment and delight of life without the aid of some kind of stimulus or excitement becomes almost impossible, and you wonder where the delicious feeling has gone of the aliveness of your youth. It hasn't gone; you've just covered it over with fear — hardened emotion.

Do you recognise in yourself what I have just described?

In love, you become especially self-guarding. You give so much of yourself but never all because you are afraid — though what of you're not quite sure. You're just afraid, cautious, holding back.

And when you do give yourself, as much as you are able, you get hurt again — because you continue to choose your partners through the emotions of your unhappy-body. Inevitably you choose unhappiness.

The unhappy-body is devoid of love and in any relationship it looks to get the love and happiness it does not have.

Since you can't receive what you can't give, the partnership of unhappy-bodies invariably ends in both people crying out in pain, or demanding love — emotional strife and torment. Or the alliance ends in a wishy-washy or painful compromise — a callous denial of love and life cosily called comfort, convenience, compatability or companionship.

Sooner or later your love life is disastrous.

Your tender dreams of love and romance are consistently punctured, bruised and violated.

Each hurt, disappointment and heartbreak which in your ignorance you thought had passed, or that you'd got over, joins up with your residual unhappy-body. Here they weep and grieve again as the moods and depressions you can't explain, yet cling to as yourself.

3
UNHAPPINESS BEGINS NOW

To rid yourself of unhappiness you must first prevent any more unhappiness from gathering in you.

Unhappiness is substantial and it gathers now. Any unhappiness you remember and grieve over is already past and resident in you. So that is not the unhappiness that begins now.

Unhappiness begins with events which are immediately identifiable, events like crashing your car, being parted from someone you love, a sexual disaster, a death, losing your job — any sort of shock.

The task is to prevent the emotion of the moment from entering you. This requires immediate action in that instant.

First action is to face the fact that the event has actually happened.

The initial reaction normally is one of disbelief. This is an attempt by the unhappy-body to escape or look away from the reality in order to avoid shock. This allows time for emotion to rush in — and you lose your presence.

So you must first perceive the fact.

You do this by not seeing the event as a problem, that is, by not thinking what it will mean to you in the future or how it is going to affect you.

You must stay in the present. You must be real. And to be real means to be present where you are at the moment.

The future has not come. The fact is that your car or part of your life is changed in front of you. Don't interpret. Don't analyse. You must see the event only as it is without putting any imagination or conclusions onto it. Then any physical action required of you will immediately occur in your awareness — without your having to worry or think.

It is now alone that matters. The instant you leave the present by thinking about the future or the past you will be unhappy. You will allow emotion in. That applies also to after the event. You must not think back on it, must not go over it in your mind.

The shock of the event at the time cannot be avoided. But shock is not emotion.

Shock is a vacuum — the vacuum in which self-change can occur. Shock cuts out all thought, all continuity of the past in you. At the moment of shock, you are new — if you can be present. And the possibility of fundamental, radical self-change is enormous. The panic and worry only starts when you allow thoughts to re-enter and stir up the old emotional body permitting more emotion, more unhappiness to pour in.

You must keep to action moment to moment, as

dictated by the energy of the event itself. See the event, the scene itself and you will see with clarity what has to be done, if anything.

Don't do what you think. Do what is right. And what is right is reflected in what is — the event as it is in the world now in front of you — not in your imagination. If nothing is to be done you will see that, so then do nothing. But don't think.

If you allow your mind to move outside the now by projecting into the future or past — even reflecting on what someone might say or think — you will turn the incident into a problem. It will then no longer be perceived for what it is — a pure happening. You will have injected fear, your emotional unhappiness, into it.

If you can keep it as a pure happening by not conceiving it to be what it is not, it will not cause you unhappiness — now or in the future. Keep the unhappiness out now and you keep it out of the future. Other events flowing from the incident will then fall into place rightly — in their own moment.

But if you are feeling emotional pain it means you are not seeing straight. You have short-circuited yourself, cut off from the natural flow. You are thinking, projecting your fears and uncertainties — your emotional body — onto the event. The event will then have to reflect some of the same unhappy emotions back to you in subsequent events, which will then appear to contain more of the same problem.

In the next few paragraphs I am going to explain just what this means and the truth behind it.

It is one of the great liberating truths of existence. To connect energetically with it in yourself, you may have to read the explanation over several times, and at more than one sitting. But when you make the connection it will release great self-knowledge or spiritual clarity.

Here it is.

Everything happens in your consciousness. That is how you are conscious of what happens.

What you imagine to have happened, such as what happened while you were asleep last night, is an entirely different thing. That is the working of the mind, not of consciousness. Consciousness is behind the mind and it provides the consciousness that allows the mind to work and reflect. The mind is dependent on the consciousness. But consciousness is not dependent on the mind.

Let me give you another example of the difference between the two in your daily life.

If your car is crashed *in your absence* by another driver, the event did not occur in your consciousness. The event in that case occurs in your consciousness only at the moment you are informed of it. And how you react or respond to it in that moment determines whether you make a problem of it, and create for yourself a succession of problems to follow.

In other words the clarity with which you are able to perceive an event, determines how the events and the circumstances flowing from it will affect you in the future.

If an event is seen as a problem when it happens, whatever happens afterwards in that connection will be seen as an extension of the same problem, and will in fact become a part of the same problem.

Which means the event will be followed by a succession of other problematical events — such as, if you crash your car, the problem of getting the damaged vehicle to a garage, being without the car for several weeks, finding the money to pay the insurance excess and so on.

This normal problematical sequence of living, humanity has come to accept as the unquestionable natural flow of events: every problem requires other problems, or time and effort, to solve it.

But this is not the truth. And it is not natural or necessary at all.

It is indeed what generally happens, but only because everyone creates problems in their consciousness out of events. Once you cease doing this, once you begin seeing each event as unique in this moment and having no problematical continuity or future, the entire dynamic changes.

This is because of the power of your consciousness.

Your consciousness — not your mind — is the most powerful, creative thing in existence.

It directs your life from behind the mind — completely faithful to how you perceive life. It does not force anything on you: it creates for you, according to the clarity of your perception. For you are in charge of your life and how you see life is how it affects you, or how it must be.

If you perceive problems, your consciousness is compelled to create problems.

If, however, you start to resist problem-making and see events only as they happen, then your consciousness is free to begin working naturally, as it is supposed to, without any more problems being created.

This is the miracle of life, the miracle of consciousness, that eliminates all unhappiness.

Now let me give you the key to it all.

The truth which makes this miracle possible is that every event that happens in your consciousness is the natural answer or solution to a previous event.

Any delay or problem is only in the mind.

It means, that if you do not give an event a future as having an effect in time, by thinking it's going to be a problem or cause a problem, any seeming difficulty will be quickly cancelled out by some other event. All you have to do is BE — and the solution will arrive.

To illustrate: if you crash your car, a tow-truck comes around the corner or someone offers you a tow; someone out-of-the-blue lends you a car while yours is being repaired; you receive a sum of money you weren't expecting to pay the insurance excess. Whatever the situation, there are no problems: because you are not making them.

All you have to do is respond to events as they occur and keep the emotional problem-making out of your consciousness by not reacting anxiously or impatiently to them. What is necessary will be provided by the natural unfolding of events.

The secret is that the less you make a problem of your life — any event in your life — the less time or emotion is created between the event and its natural solution.

In short, you reduce and finally eliminate time as a difficulty or restriction.

Events then flow timelessly and the life is sweet, easy and effortless — even though to others it may seem to be a problem.

It all comes down to this: you make the problem, you magnify it, and then you think that in time or by your actions you dissolve or solve it.

When all you are doing, with all your worrying and frustration, is delaying the solution which would have come earlier, anyway.

There is no problem in the first place.

You — your unhappiness that prevents you from seeing the simple truth of life — are the only problem.

You, the problem-maker, merely get in the way as the pain and confusion of it all.

Rid yourself of the problem, your unhappiness, and all problems — all unhappiness — disappears.

4
DISSOLVING THE GROWTH

Starting to dissolve the emotional self that has built up in you since birth is a big job.

It is a harder road for some than for others. Sometimes it takes only a few words like these to communicate the whole idea: the man or woman immediately sees what has to be done and starts getting on with it with a tremendous feeling of relief and discovery.

To start, you have to be able to feel the presence of your emotional self within you. Unless you feel it you can't begin to deal with it. When it is rampant and active, such as when you are angry or depressed, it is likely to be too powerful for you to remain separate from; you will become identified with it, absorbed by it and lose yourself in it.

So you must begin to identify the emotional body in normal times, like now, when it is probably just dormant, ticking over. Unless you have become sufficiently still through right meditation — and not all meditation is right — you will have difficulty discerning it.

The surface of your emotional self can be felt now by closing your eyes and focussing your inner attention on the feeling, the sensation, in the stomach area. This means feeling the actual feeling, the physical sensation, inside your body.

All your moods and depressions rise up from the subconscious through that sensation.

If you have just had an argument, the emotional stress will be felt there first in the abdomen around the navel. But the stress will spread quickly through the whole of your body — especially to the heart, chest, throat and eventually the head where it will create a headache, tiredness, confusion or some other distracting reaction.

The emotional body is as alive and intelligent as you are. It does not want to be found out — to be seen to be separate from your true self. It will try to distract you — and usually succeeds.

One way it does this is to affect other parts of the body with aches and pains. These, however, will not be lasting because the emotional body does not have the endurance, the staying power, to affect any area for more than an hour or so at a time. But it will keep bringing back the aches and pains.

Its main distraction, to prevent you from getting at the root of it in your belly and starting to dissolve it, is to make you think.

You must understand that due to your neglect and ignorance, the emotional unhappy-body has taken charge of much of your inner self, your subconscious. It will not surrender. You have to get in there, consciously or energetically, and root it out.

To dissolve the unhappy-body requires action now.

You must make a start somewhere, and now — this moment — is always where you begin.

You start by pausing at the end of this paragraph, closing your eyes, being as still and silent as you can within, and feeling the feeling, the physical *sensation* in your body around the belly.

What you are feeling is IT — your residual emotion, the unhappy tenant of your body.

It may seem harmless and very ordinary now if you are not disturbed. But once you're upset, it will be an intense feeling, a compulsive urge to worry or do something other than focus on the discomfort of the feeling.

If at this moment you cannot feel the feeling of yourself, it means you are not still enough and are unlikely to make any real progress until you learn to meditate rightly.

Again, immediate action is required: arrange to learn right meditation.

While focussing on sensation, do not think about what you are doing. Just do it.

Thinking means projecting into the future or back into the past — distraction.

The emotion itself makes you think like that. It knows that while you are thinking you are dissipating the only energy that can destroy it — your conscious attention.

Look energetically. You do this by holding the

sensation with your attention. Perceive it, feel what is there. Don't draw conclusions. Conclusions are thinking, not looking. Looking energetically like this with the attention is seeing, discovering what is — without putting a name to it.

The beautiful simplicity and effectiveness of this process is the most difficult thing for people to grasp. Because of their unhappy-bodies people are complicated. They can't see straight because they can't look straight. They look for problems and miss the simple solution in front of them.

The simple truth here is that your conscious attention, once focussed on the inner feeling of yourself, will destroy whatever is false in that feeling.

Since emotion or unhappiness is the falsehood in you — because it turns to pain — it is gradually dissolved or destroyed.

What is left behind is the true — your joyous, natural, vibrant self, your happy body. This can never be annihilated because it alone is real in you. As the false is destroyed you come alive.

So let me restate the practical side of the process and take it a little further.

Whether you are peaceful, or agitated after a blazing row — and especially later if you are upset or angered by anything in this book — sit down and focus your inner attention on the feeling in your navel area — and hold it.

Then, when you've got hold of it, sink into it, sink into that feeling.

It will try to throw you off, like the momentum of a spinning disc. Stay with it. Lower yourself, your attention, into it. Become it, become the feeling, the sensation. But without thinking.

You do this simply by being still. Stillness is your only strength against this extraordinary opponent within you. Stiller and stiller is the way. Stillness alone can get into it, penetrate it. Only stillness, the stillness of your perception, your conscious awareness undisturbed by thought or consideration, has the power to dissolve the accumulated discontent, pain and restlessness that is there.

As you succeed you will feel pain, fear, doubt — and threatened. This will be the old concealed emotions themselves rising up through you and being dissolved as they are being faced up to.

The unhappy-body will writhe, complain, cry, ache and try to scream through your body.

It will do anything to make you run away, to remove your searing conscious attention from it. It will try to force you to get up and move about, to grab a drink, go out, to convince you that you or I are mad, to make you declare the whole thing is pointless and give up.

But you must hold.

You must hold your body still as long as you possibly can. Then move around if you must; take a break for ten minutes — and sit down and start again. Do not give up.

When I say hold your body still I do not mean suppress it. It is the cornered emotion that will move your body at these times. By holding the emotion itself, it will be powerless to make your body move. Emotion cannot move while you are focussed on it.

The emotional unhappy-body is a living thing — living off you like a parasite — and it does not want to die.

But that is what is happening. You are killing it, killing all your painful and lonely past with your awareness of the present.

Section Two

THE HARDEST
DEATH

The earth is beautiful, joyous, cosmic, eternal.
There are no problems on earth.

The world is the unhappy superstructure man
has imposed on earth.
The world consists of his problems.

Both earth and world are within you.

What you see outside and how it affects you is
purely the reflection of what is within you.
If you see and feel beauty in your life it is the
earth, the life within you, that you are perceiving.
If you see problems and feel unhappy in your life
you are looking at the world, not the earth.

To reach the immortality of life on earth within
you, you have to dissolve your attachment to the world.
That attachment is devilishly subtle.
Any mental or emotional pain you feel at any
time is it.
You must see this — and not try to water it down
by making exceptions and excuses as the world in you
will do. You must face the pain in you, the world in you
without running away into justifications. There are no
justifications for unhappiness, none whatever.

To remove any room in you for doubt and interpretations I will repeat that fundamental truth: any mental or emotional pain you feel at any time in your life, irrespective of the cause, is due to the world in you. You have left the earth and are concentrating on the world.

You must see through the world by recognising it for what it is — what it has done to you and what it is doing to you; as you must see through yourself by recognising that your pain or confusion is your love of the world.

The world is only ever as pressing a problem as your love of it.

By stillness and with courage you must descend to the bottom of the world in you and then through the bottom of the world in you.

That is hell — for a while.

But it is your hell, no one else's — the hell you have been pleased to make for yourself on earth by believing in the world and attaching yourself to its values, its ways and the things and persons in it, all of which were always going to leave you or elude you, anyway.

Anything you love in the world will cause you pain.

That pain is the hell you must pass through — either now, or in the process of your physical death.

Go through hell rightly and you reunite with the changeless beauty and joy of the earth in yourself as yourself.

And in spite of all your worldly dreads and fears,

you lose nothing.

Go through hell wrongly and you go round in circles making more problems, more world without end, more hell for yourself.

Be still and know that I am hell.
Do not complain. Be valiant.
Be still and know that I am just.
Be patient.
Be still and know that I am God.
For I am God, the spirit of the earth beneath the world in you.
When you know me in your stillness you are one with the joy of life on earth and one with me.
Come.
Be still.
Listen.
Take no thought.
Descend into yourself.
Come back to earth, come back to life.
Descend into me.

Section Two
part one

DYING TO
THE WORLD

6
LIKES AND DISLIKES

You must now die consciously to your likes and dislikes, to your attachment to them.

This is the hardest death of all.

The daily pain, conflict and confusion of the world is the unconscious interaction of likes and dislikes. The daily pain, conflict and confusion of the spiritual way is the conscious dying to them.

Likes and dislikes are the fluctuating feelings that sit on top of and shut out the awareness of your natural true feeling of life — the unwavering joy or bliss of being alive, or simply being.

People make the error of thinking they are in this state by just being their normal self. But they overlook the unhappiness — the intermittent depressions, moods and problems — they voluntarily carry around with them as part of their normal personal self or life.

The state of being is distinguished by being at all times in the unshakeable joy or bliss of life within —

no unhappiness. And this, by the miracle of the life or self made right as the individual man or woman, is reflected externally by the absence of any problems in the world.

As within, so without.

Only when the attachment to your likes and dislikes is dissolved for all time, can you be — be yourself.

This is the end of existence or karma as a burden.

The spiritual process of detachment from your likes and dislikes requires you first to hear and understand the enormity of what you are dealing with at every level of yourself and your existence.

This is the purpose of this middle section of the book.

And then it requires you to apply that understanding to the reality of your daily life moment to moment, within and without, as your own self-knowledge.

The last section of the book will be your energetic reminder of that.

★

Being is in pure sensation.

And being in pure sensation is a distinctly blissful, self-sustaining feeling — what the original Sanskrit-speaking sages of India called ananda. It does not vary or end. It is the pure feeling of life as the sensation or perception of yourself free of dependence on the world or attachment to it.

When you feel anything but easy in your sensation you are feeling the disturbance in the next level up, the next stratum or layer of yourself.

Here, the sensation is no longer one pure feeling.

It contains many different, changing feelings.

This level of emotion, this substratum, is your false self.

It consists of a now hard-set emotional sediment — a bed rock — of all your hurts, disappointments and frustrations since childhood that you have not faced up to.

This unhappy core of yourself acts like a gong. Through it reverberates the emotional interplay — the excitement, good and bad — of your likes and dislikes which you register as your changing feelings or moods.

This false self lies under the surface in your subconscious.

And the only part of it that shows for you to start to consciously or spiritually get a hold of and deal with in your daily life, are its two opposing poles of your liking and disliking.

These, if you watch closely and are still enough, stick up in your awareness like two harmless-looking mountain peaks. They are always there but have become so much the scenery of yourself that you don't even notice them any more, let alone know them or feel them to be intrusive or menacing.

They are in fact seething volcanoes. And they give no overt sign of the residual emotion or force of unhappiness linking them underneath that periodically explodes, making your life a misery, or someone else's life a misery through you.

Let me ask you a question that most people have pondered on at some time or other.

How did the individual Nazi men and women

muster sufficient inhumanity of feeling to inflict such unspeakable atrocities on their completely helpless victims?

Or the Japanese on their equally helpless prisoners-of-war?

Or any other national or partisan group since, on any other helpless group of people or individuals?

How are any of us able to inflict on one another and other life-forms the cruelties that all are guilty of?

All violence, hatred and inhumanity arise from that subconscious substratum of old ingrained personal pain and falsehood — the residual unhappiness that is in everyone.

7

HAPPY TO BE UNHAPPY

From birth, everyone — you now — is compelled and encouraged by the emotional ignorance of parents, teachers and society to attach themselves to their likes and dislikes and to identify with them.

From the first moment of apparent comprehension, the child — you now — is taught to "like this" to "like that"; to react with pleasure or excitement to outside stimulation.

(Similarly, this gives pleasure or excitement at the same time to the parent — yesterday's child still in the making.)

What is not realised is that as the child (or adult) learns to attach itself to the pleasant excited feeling of what it likes — what it will call "good" — it is automatically attaching itself to the opposite negative painful excitation of what it does not like — the inevitable cessation of the "good" feeling when the object is removed.

This feeling it will call "bad" — and the feeling will be registered as depression, anger, frustration, discontent or boredom.

This means:

- *When you embrace what you like you embrace what you are not going to like in the future.*

   To the degree that anything you like excites you at any time, you will have to suffer the same degree of negative excitement by something you do not like at a later time.

   "Liking" and "disliking" are one whole entity — as the two ends of a fence are the one fence. But in time, the beginning and end must follow each other, whichever end you start from.

   Pleasure must end in pain and pain must end in the relief of pain, pleasure. "Good" must follow "bad" and "bad" must follow "good" with the inevitability that day follows night and night follows day.

- *Liking and disliking are precisely the same excitement or stimulation of the emotions. Except that one has a plus or positive quality and the other a minus or negative quality.*

   They are still the two ends of the same vibrant animal — one the tail of the animal which is relatively harmless and often soft and caressing, and the other the head which bites.

   When you play with any part of the animal you play with both ends.

- *The excitement of liking and disliking is identical with the stimulation of pleasure AND unhappiness — and they are artificially induced.*

They are actually a device resorted to by humanity to try to find a substitute for the vanishing feeling of the natural joy of life, or one's true self within.

Once the ability or sensitivity to feel the sweetness of life within is lost you have to have a substitute and that is what excitement is. It creates an artificial feeling of life on which everyone gets hooked.

So from birth, the infant child's whole attention — your attention — is focussed on the artificially stimulated feeling of what in the world pleases it or does not please it.

Until finally it succumbs to the self-delusion that life — the feeling of being alive — is identical with the feeling of liking: "I feel pleasure — I feel alive. Give me more pleasure — and I feel more life."

But adult and child, in their ignorance, are unable to perceive the other half of the equation — or that which is going on in the subconscious beneath their surface awareness.

Here, the awareness is: "When I feel pleasure I feel alive. And when I feel pain *I also feel alive.* Pleasure or pain, good or bad, give me the feeling of life." So at this level, I do not care whether it is pleasure or pain I feel. All that matters is that I feel alive — and pleasure or pain, the good or the bad, give me that feeling.

And what about the wailing and the tears on the surface, the pleas for relief and protests that I do not want this unhappiness? No one wants to be unhappy, do they?

Yes. They do. When you are unhappy you want to be unhappy. Otherwise you would not be unhappy.

You cannot blame anyone or anything else. The unhappiness is in you and it is yours.

The truth is you love your unhappiness. You won't let it go. You cling to it. And your love of unhappiness is your love of the world — your attachment to what you like and dislike in it.

When you are unhappy it's always about something in the world, even if it is only your worldly dislike of yourself.

While you still love the world, are still attached to it through your likes and dislikes, you cannot feel the much finer love of life within you sufficiently to give up the attachment; so you go on needing the excitement of its pleasure and pain.

You cannot love life and the world. It is one or the other. Love of the world will obscure the love of life.

When you no longer need the world's pain you won't need its phoney pleasure either.

You will then have the natural joy of life that never ends, and no longer be dependent on the world's up-down excitement.

And yet the world will not vanish. You will still be in it, do what you do and enjoy what you do. But you will not be attached to it. You will perform better in it because you won't be unhappy. You will be able to love more. And it will no longer have the power to hurt you.

So the truth for you to see in your own daily experience from this moment is that you are happy to be unhappy as you are happy to be happy: because it is the only way that in your present though waning ignorance, you can feel alive.

In between pleasure and pain is boredom, living death — no excitation of liking or disliking, no interplay in the substratum.

But again you can only be bored because you are ignorant of yourself, have lost the natural feeling of the life in yourself.

To feel bored you must still be alive. But as you can no longer feel life within, without stimulation from without, you feel dead.

In adulthood, the child — as yourself — will again demonstrate its misunderstanding of life and lack of touch with the reality of itself in two common or popular extremes of emotional excitement.

In moments of intense pleasure it will feel or exclaim, "This is life — now I'm really living," and in moments of similarly intense disliking or depression its reaction will be, "Life is too painful: I want to die." And it might even take a knife or a poison to its own body to prove it.

Yet, even while the want is to die, still there underneath the wretched need for excitement at any price, is the joy of life that you were born with, the joy that makes the birds sing and that never ends in all its simplicity and wonder despite the unhappy wanton self.

8
IGNORANCE IN THE NURSERY

Every child — you — is born with love as the feeling of itself.

That is why a baby, without any external stimulation, will lie staring into space gurgling happily or blissfully in the sensation of its own natural joy or being within its body.

Its irresistibly delightful smiles express the constant bliss or ananda of its true self that it is feeling.

And it would continue to consciously be in touch with this feeling for the rest of its days but for the ignorance of its parents and society.

The parents, in their ignorance of their own true self and therefore of the true self of the child, set out as quickly as possible to draw the child lopsidedly out of itself towards their own unhappy, confused and lopsided condition.

With the assistance of other misguided family members, they do this by focussing the infant's entire attention onto the sounds of rattles, the sight of moving colours and twitching faces, the feeling of fabric dolls, and the physical pressure of their own loving squeezes — all of which deflect the baby's awareness from the constancy of feeling of the joy of life within its body to the passing stimulation of what happens to be happening outside.

Very rarely is there any conscious affirmation, acknowledgement and participation in the child's precious inner state or consciousness. This, by omission and neglect, dies on the vine.

Gradually, the nursery and family routine induces in the child a recognition and then a reliance on these artificially stimulated feelings of what happens to please it and does not please it in the outer world.

It forgets its true self — leaves it by becoming unconscious of it — and begins looking for sensory excitement as a way of living.

When what pleases it is missing — or there is no one around to shake the rattle, make funny faces or generally excite it with their company — the child has less and less within to fall back on, less and less inward joy that needs no stimulation. The child becomes increasingly discontented, lonely, unhappy — emotional, demanding, wanting without knowing what it wants.

Previously the child was content to be with its own love within itself, given its natural physical needs. Now it requires constant, growing reassurance — emotional love, the outer world's hot and cold substitute for true-self love. Mother love, though not always reliable, is the best of this.

The child that was spiritually individual and free, is now emotionally dependent, an emotional captive of the world, a miniature carbon copy of the rest of the unhappy human race.

9

HUMAN LOVE: ITS WEAKNESS AND ITS PAIN

Emotional love or human love is the love that cries over lost objects or persons.

It is a love that brings pain and heartbreak — so it is not natural and not fulfilling for long.

Breaking consciously with this love, which is part of dying to your likes and dislikes, is as painful when it happens as losing everything you have ever loved.

But then, love itself floods in.

Emotional or human love arises from liking and disliking.

It is induced into the child by normal upbringing until finally love and contentment are associated only with outer perceptions and confirmations.

So when a loved object or connection is removed the child feels it has lost its love.

Even the crying over a broken toy is a demonstration of this.

And later, the child as you the adult, will

frequently demonstrate the point again amidst much weeping and unhappiness: when someone or something you love dies or departs the heartfelt cry will be, "My love is dead — I am desolate." Or, "My love has left me — I can't go on."

None of which is the truth.

Your love is always within.

Your love is within for you to feel now precisely as it was when you were a baby alone and gurgling contentedly in your cradle — before your parents and guardians, in their loneliness and unhappiness, started to excite you as a means of exciting themselves.

Emotional or human love is selfish.

Because of its coarseness you can no longer constantly and consciously feel your selfless love — although at times you will indeed touch this within and be filled with the wonder of yourself.

The exquisite fineness of your selfless love is obscured by excitable dependence since birth on having to see it reflected in some external form or knowledge.

You are unable to take love direct and pure as itself. You want a reflection of it, not the love as it is.

You have lost your sensitivity to the purity — the unknowable energy — of love.

Pure love is unselfish because it does not need to take a single thing from anyone. For you to feel it, to be it, no one has to even exist — and so endure the pains of existence for you; no one has to be with you — and so possibly be apart from someone else who needs them.

It is utterly undemanding of anything or anyone in the world — for it is complete in itself, in you. And yet it is not selfish nor ignorant — in its completeness and unendingness, it ensures that there is no unhappiness in you to make others unhappy. That is love.

At the same time this love will also ensure that individuals and conditions appear outside of you to reflect your love, for you to love. Where you are they will be. But when they go, as all things must, they will not break your heart. Love, the same love that is within you, will always come again in form.

If you are a parent and truly love your child you will make it your selfless loving responsibility to keep the child in contact with its original consciousness and the sweet feeling of itself.

With a new-born baby, this is done from the first moment it lies in your arms by speaking directly to it in straightforward language and loving tones. You speak to it about the wonder and knowledge of life and love, and the keeping of unhappiness out of yourself that you have discovered from reading this book and applying the truths of it in your daily life.

You speak from your own self-knowledge, your own integrity.

As you practise addressing the child in this way you will find it increasingly easy to maintain an intelligent and meaningful communication between you. It might seem at first like a monologue. But gradually you will realise it is an extraordinary dialogue, that the child is silently — energetically — responding to every word from its inner selfless consciousness, its love.

Mothers tend to do this naturally with their new-born. But due to our material times and their own unhappiness and lack of real knowledge of life and love, the expression is no longer conscious enough, real enough in them to be sustained.

You must understand that the communication I am describing is energetic.

It is not dependent on words, although the sound of your words will actually carry the conscious speechless energy of your love that communicates direct to the child's consciousness or love.

Continue the dialogue right through the child's life. It won't be long before the child begins to speak verbally itself and you can then converse increasingly together in words about the truth of life and love that you have found, within and without. The child's frontal awareness and perceptions of the world will then be in tune with the energy of its real self. Its development then will not be lopsided.

The child will have much to communicate and say that utterly astounds you. You will find it responding from an amazing place within far more real and profound than its years.

You will grow in love and truth and life together. For that is what parenthood and childhood are for.

10
PSYCHIC POSSESSION

In normal upbringing, when the child first starts to talk, the false self seated in the subconscious rises and gains a recognisable ascendancy.

The likes and dislikes begin speaking through the child.

There is then the child itself who speaks — the same delightful self-contented child who smiled and gurgled in the baby's crib — and the other restless, unhappy thing that speaks.

Both use the same body.

Only one is real.

But the parents and closest adults, by conversing with the child's likes and dislikes and entertaining them with false notions of love and kindness, give the invading emotion human status or recognition.

This is disastrous.

The likes and dislikes then start assuming an independent emotional identity and false authority.

This is centred in the throat.

Unsuspected by all because it is the norm, the child is being taken over.

It is being emotionally — psychically — possessed.

Inevitably and tragically, the parents accept or tolerate the degenerative emotion as part of the child itself.

From its seat in the throat the emotion gradually invades every cell in the body. It is a slow process, immensely accelerated and strengthened by puberty, as described in Section One.

The child itself is powerless to resist the psychic invader.

At this stage, its one hope is to have the supporting strength and authority of a parent or guardian whose love has been made real enough by the absence of unhappiness in themselves.

Due to our times this has been extremely rare. But there is more chance of it happening now through you.

Such a parent, being sufficiently one with their own life and love within can stand fast as surrogate for the child and consciously face the emotion. This is not a fight or battle with the child although it might be perceived as one.

It is done by pure presence, by confronting the unhappy psychic invader with the only authority it will yield to or cannot bear — an utterly unemotional, unexcitable presence of love. This is love beyond acquisition or human understanding — in short, love free of the distractions of liking and disliking, selfless love.

As things are in the world, however, the emotion

in the child is invariably faced with human love — love dependent on the stimulation of external perceptions, good and bad. This love itself is emotional. It gets sucked into a psychic vortex and contributes to the force of the possession through its own psychic possession. It does not have the essential endurance — the power to resist a compromise with the invader, usually in the name of "love".

The result is that the growing child's habitual verbal declarations and posturings of what it likes and does not like — what it wants and does not want — although at times infuriating to its loving elders, are quietly accepted for better and for worse as its perfectly normal, tolerable and intolerable, contradictory human self.

The child can now be said to be shaping up nicely to take its place in the rest of the perfectly normal tormented and tormenting unhappy world.

In later life, this automatic acceptance into the human fold of the child's contradictory self will inevitably create problems for it, and society.

But as everyone is living the same way who is to say it is contradictory?

For example, when the emotion or liking of patriotism excites him (or her) to go and kill someone for his country, he will be praised and his action highly commended. But when the same emotion of liking or disliking excites him to kill or injure someone at another time, he will be censured and locked up; or in more emotionally assertive societies he will be executed.

Never will he really get over the confusion of such contradictory justice. But he will try to live with it for better and for worse as society will try to live with him.

If on the other hand the child as an adult is to be freed of unhappiness and confusion, a more real parent or guardian will come along and point the way which the original parents and guardians could not do.

This will be the teacher of truth.

His presence and words will cause a good deal of pain. In adulthood the possessing psychic entity is well and truly entrenched as the unhappy contradictory personality itself, and the only pain in fact and truth is its destruction.

The pain that is suffered — and the disruptions that occur in the life to help bring about the pain — will be in proportion to how much the individual longs to be free.

And so will be the floodings of joy, wonder and love that occur in between.

Longing is not wanting.

Everybody wants to be free, but few long for it. Wanting has innumerable objects. But longing is for life, for freedom which has no object. You just long for what you do not know and cannot name.

The teacher of truth is surrogate for the head of the human family, the one parent, the one God or the one life or good that knows no unhappiness in time, and whose joy it is that you should real-ise this in yourself, as yourself.

11
THE RESPONSIBLE PARENT

By now the young child's original finer feeling of sweet inner self-fulfilment is slowly disappearing under the crude weight of acquired excitability, impatience and discontent.

Coming in fast are the frustrations and anxieties of wanting what it likes and cannot have, and not wanting what it has.

The periods in which it can "just be" — alone and performing without entertainment — are shorter and fewer.

To feel that it is alive it has now to like or not like what it is doing — instead of simply being and doing. Especially, it has to feel the excitement and psychic tension created in the presence of others of declaring through the wilful throat centre what it likes and dislikes.

If you are a responsible parent or teacher you will not converse with the child's likes and dislikes.

You will not allow the child to say what it likes or does not like. You will guide it into finding other words to express its preferences so that the selfish force of liking and disliking does not get expression through the voice.

Neither will you allow the exclamation, "I want" or "I don't want". And you will have no discussion with the wanting or not-wanting energy.

You will not do any of this by ignorant force and suppression. You will avoid those and yet still be able to punish the child as necessary by explaining to it in its still and receptive periods what you are both confronting and precisely how and what you are doing. This alone produces enduring trust and authority.

If you have contributed your wisdom and consciousness to the child since birth, as I described earlier, it will be no shock to it what you are doing and why it is being done. In fact, the child will be your collaborator. For you will have informed it long ago of the one and only danger that faces all human beings coming into existence. It will know all about the psychic invader and much of what is in this book. You will have demonstrated much of it in the child's own experience — the most powerful instruction possible.

The longer you have left it, the harder it is going to be.

You must learn to recognise the first sign of the emotion rising to express itself in the child.

This will be a seemingly harmless word, reaction or gesture. At that moment you must immediately confront both child and emotion, alerting the child to what is coming (mood or unhappiness) and to be ready for it.

Your approach must always be that you are doing it together. "We (you and the child) will not have it in us, will we?" And although the failures are almost incessant, you must keep going. For if you are going to save the child you must also save yourself — by keeping the moods and unhappiness out of yourself.

Remember, for both the child and yourself there is no failure: just endeavour to do better next time and don't dwell on the past.

The child has to be led to see the invader for what it is: something separate from itself, an unhappy emotion that it — the happy, untroubled child — does not want so therefore will not hold onto.

You must be very firm and very strong; patient, present, emotionless and wise.

12
THE FAMILY AND SOCIAL EXAMPLE

The growing child's descent — your descent — into ignorance and unhappiness is fostered throughout by family life.

Unsuspected, the psychic possession continues.

Family life with its celebrations of birthdays, Christmas, anniversaries, material gift-giving and the constant fuelling of the child's expectations of future pleasure and rewards, insidiously affirms and dignifies identification with the invading false self.

By the example and indulgence of parents, the child learns to state and restate what it likes and does not like as supposedly genuine expressions of itself — and to defend and justify these acquired posturings with righteous and outraged vehemence.

It also learns from example to accept that the strife and unhappiness this causes is normal and even necessary to family life — and love.

Most unfortunately of all, it learns from elders

to believe that it has the right to be unhappy, moody and ill-tempered — and that as these are natural to human beings so they can be forgiven or excused in oneself.

Meanwhile, the parents' own underlying unhappiness is demonstrated for the child to absorb into its subconscious by their almost complete dependence on liking and disliking as a way of life. Their most memorable experiences and main topics of conversation are based on what they like and do not like.

The child is continuously exposed to conversations like this:

"Did you have a good (exciting or get-what-you-like) time on the holiday you were looking forward (for excitement) to?"

"Yes, it was interesting (not so exciting) but it was very depressing (negatively exciting) when..... How have you been?"

"We've been well (meaning physically — no mention of love of the beauty or truth of life) but John is unhappy (negatively excited) about his job. He had a wonderful (exciting) promotion but....."

"What did you do yesterday?" (The questioner is looking for excitement, not love or life).

"Nothing much (no excitement). But tonight we're having a dinner party (excitement to look forward to, and more conversations like this one about likes and dislikes)."

Apart from the influence of their friends, the parents' attachment to their false and unhappy selves — the possessing psychic identity — is kept alive and vibrant for them by society's relentless stimulation of their likes and dislikes. This is done through the exciting propaganda of the advertising agencies, along with the likes and dislikes — or opinions of what is emotionally and sensationally meaningful — of the news, information and entertainment media.

In everyone's daily life there is virtually no reference whatever to the joy and bliss of just being alive without the stimulation or excitement of some activity or problem.

The whole waking life of child, family and society is directed towards artificially generating the excitement of liking or pleasure; or stimulating the (exciting) fear of losing it.

Drinks, food, music, recreation, fashion, furnishings, religious beliefs, personality, nursery stories, books, films, friends, associates are all chosen on the basis of who or what stirs, or is hoped will stir, a sensational feeling of liking or pleasure.

And the threatened loss of these things excites the opposite feeling of disliking or displeasure.

Gambling, competition and even illicit love affairs owe their attraction to the exciting stimulus of possible loss as much as to possible gain.

Everything is centred on the perceived body, the senses and their functions.

In childhood the identification starts with what is happening to the child's own body or person. Then it extends to what is happening to others and eventually to the whole world.

Useless involvement, useless curiosity and hypocritical concern increase in proportion to the growing number of things, people and conditions to like and dislike.

It is kicks — stimulation, good or bad, all the way.

Tears alternate with laughter, excitement with depression. And finally, as it all began in the initial pleasure (or pain) of birth and hope, so it all ends in the final pain and disappointment (or relief) of death.

Poets and dreamers of the race, feeling the presence of the one life but never managing to consciously find it, present the contorted living process as something majestic and dignified — when it is an avoidable obscenity, the artificially induced throes of unhappiness imposed upon a whole species by wilful ignorance of itself.

The steady, unchanging reality of bliss and joy that lies in the natural being under the acquired excitability, remains unperceived and seldom consciously approached or addressed.

Anything approximating a conscious inner sensation is likely to be limited to sexual, auditory or gastronomical stimulation; or to the feeling of physical hunger, physical pain or emotional dejection.

For any accidental inner awareness in this society, there is only one resort — the doctor.

The love, the being, the peace of self that absorbs all problems, is unknown.

13
ENTER THE UGLINESS

After the child begins to talk a distinct intermittent ugliness creeps into it.

When the ugliness is there even the most devoted parent finds it hard to believe that this is the offspring they love or gave birth to.

The child scowls. It frowns. Darkness is there. It grimaces, defies and wilfully ignores.

Cunning appears in the eyes.

The look sometimes is so old, so knowing of its own perversity that it is impossible to reconcile it with a child.

It demands — emotionally, senselessly, mindlessly.

The ferocity of its unhappiness is sometimes diabolical.

It screams, working itself up into near hysteria.

It writhes, rolls its eyes demented-like.

And occasionally you can catch its sly detached

and knowing glance looking out to confirm that it is getting the emotional reaction it wants, and feeds off, from anyone in the vicinity.

It lives off reaction.

Sympathy, anger, sentiment, disgust, repulsion — any emotion at all will satisfy and nourish it so that in its own good time it will be free to rise again.

The force of its unhappiness is pitiless, unmerciful to both child and parent.

The child is left exhausted afterwards, drained and unable to comprehend what has happened to it, apart from perhaps its memory of the helpless parent's anger or fury.

The ugliness, when it is there, exploits patience, tolerance and love.

It actually wants punishment — and raw experience of it — so it inflames others and gets what it wants. It drives mother and father to violence of mood or action that they never believed they were capable of. Then it howls and screams because it wants what it does not have — an end of the punishment.

What it does not have it wants. What it does have it does not want. Nothing can pacify or satisfy it.

It demands love and understanding and crucifies love and understanding.

It injects guilt like venom into those who react to it: and despair into those who would try to comfort or heal it.

It does not know what it wants because it already has what it wants, itself. It is pure unhappiness.

It is that which likes-and-does-not-like coming into existence once again to make life on earth a misery.

The fiendish force is the living emotion, the living

intelligence of psychic unhappiness that enters and possesses every infant through the ignorance of the world.

And it lives in the subconscious of every man and woman until rooted out by conscious confrontation.

14
THE AWFUL TRUTH

No one knows that every child is being psychically possessed because everyone who could know is themselves psychically possessed.

Occasionally, people vaguely perceive the psychic possession in others.

But the full extent of it — the enormity of it — cannot be comprehended until the individual themselves has cleared his or her own psychic space of the invading evil.

Only then is the man or woman spiritually, or consciously strong enough, to face the awful truth: society, the whole world, is possessed.

Society, comprising the entire man-made world, is the working model of universal psychic possession or force.

And this in spite of the learned psychiatrists and psychologists who are all unhappy — and so possessed.

Old superstitions in whose name attempts were

made to rid others of evil spirits by various tortures and "cures", were partial perceptions of the truth of possession. But as the perceptions were psychically distorted in the perceivers themselves the truth was not seen as being a universal possession.

Inevitably, the "evil" was perceived only in others, not in oneself.

On occasions when the possession was seen in oneself — which is the first real step towards eliminating it — the individual concerned invariably regarded it as a sign of his or her own madness.

But who am I — the madness I see in me, or I who am perceiving the madness in me?

This error of accepting the madness and not the perceiver as oneself was again due to the psychic distortion inherent in all. And today this same mistake continues to be the main impediment to seeing the truth, living it and then being it.

Another fact, which also applies today, was that no one free enough of psychic possession was apparently around to inform the sufferer of the truth and thus help him or her to free themselves.

Today, rationalisation — intellectualising — of the possessing emotional energy has debunked and made unpopular the old "evil spirit" approach. But in no way has it reduced the actuality and reality of the psychic possession of everyone.

Despite the learned and professional rationalisations, the almost total psychic possession of the human race continues unabated.

And it is reflected in the universal unhappiness of every man and woman — expressing itself as worry, fear, argument, heartbreak, doubt, violence, guilt, loneliness, lack of love, poverty, exploitation, business and war in any name or form.

What the rational or scientific mind does not perceive is that emotional possession — which it might accept as a term describing someone who is angry, jealous or seething with hatred — is the same as psychic possession.

Emotional possession is psychic possession — possession by something that is not oneself.

But to the rational mind the word 'psychic' with its connotations of non-physical influences, is a bit too close to the truth as it is — the possession of man by a sinister force, not far removed from the old evil spirits.

So the word 'psychic', like the old expression 'evil spirits' before it, has to be rationalised — watered down — for everyone's rational acceptance, to the less meaningful and less direct word, 'emotion'.

To avoid any misunderstanding and distortion by the rational mind of what I am saying, let me repeat the point of all this: to be psychically possessed is to have unhappiness in your life.

In other words, if you continue to have unhappiness in yourself or your life at any time, you are psychically possessed.

15
WHAT HAPPENED TO LOVE

When you the adult feel love you are feeling the beautiful feeling of yourself that you were born with.

But today your perception of it is no longer pure, not clear.

You now need the stimulation or reflection of somebody or something outside you to stir that love, to bring your own self within to life so that you can feel that self again.

Whether the person or object is present or not, the fact is that the love you feel or want is already in you.

It is *not* outside you.

Even the love you are going to feel in the future for someone you've not yet met, is there, able to be felt now if you can be still enough.

But from the cradle you have been taught not to be still.

You have been taught as a way of life to leave the beautiful formless love, the stillness within, and to project your whole attention out through the senses onto myriads of forms, and myriads of constantly changing connections, not only in the world but in your head or memory.

This requires you to be always mentally on the go.

With the result that you can't stop thinking — or worrying — even when you want to unless your mind is engaged in something — and that, of course, means it is on the move.

All of which is the opposite of stillness.

Remember the rattles mentioned earlier that as a baby attracted you away from the feeling of stillness and love in yourself? The eye-catching colours, the soft teddy bears, the loving cuddles that you learned to like, to depend on and to look forward to?

Well, now they are for real. They have turned into people.

People, unlike rattles and teddy bears, consist of innumerable likes and dislikes and so are very seldom ever still, even when they're not moving. They keep you from being still and you keep them from being still. That's what makes good company — stimulation.

And when people are not with you they still keep you busy because you keep thinking about them. That in turn makes you feel as though you are feeling them — either in a good way (liking) or a bad way (disliking). Either way, you are not still. And certainly seldom are you still enough to feel yourself, your love, direct — without some medium between.

The difficulty with people is that they soon turn

from the company you like into the person you love.

This is because the individual man or woman is the nearest reflection you can get to the image of your true self, your still, silent and patiently waiting love within.

And your attraction to what appears as the opposite sex, is your attraction to the sensual image of the other half of yourself — the other half of your patiently waiting love within — that you have projected and are vainly looking to find in some outer form that you like.

While you continue projecting your attention onto someone (or something) you like, it will gradually turn into intense attraction or love.

This feeling of love starts with liking.

And if you persist in projecting your liking by thinking about the person, that is, by giving them your attention when they are not even with you, the liking turns to love.

Then, if you cannot be with them the feeling of love soon turns to pain — the pain of wanting what you do not have. For as day follows night, liking must bring disliking as pleasure must bring pain.

You will then feel unhappy, parted from your love. And you will say love is painful.

But neither is true. You are not parted from your love: your love is within, as always. And love does not cause pain. Only ignorance causes such pain.

The pain is due to your ignorance in thinking that you are separate from your love; and to your identifying your love with an image of it outside yourself. You cry for the mirror or the reflection in it instead of being the reality, yourself, who is looking into the mirror. You see what is not the truth and suffer from not seeing the truth.

No wonder you hurt.

It is like dreaming you have lost the top half of your body and having to search through hundreds of suitcases to try to find it. When it is obvious you cannot be separate from half of yourself — unless you are dreaming.

16
LOVE, THE TEACHER

Love is real.

The love that knows pain is not real.

The pain of love — the heartbreak of lost love — is purely the negative stimulation, the dislike, of losing the object you were positively stimulated by, or liked.

As you were positively excited so you have to be negatively excited. For while you choose to be attached to liking and disliking, pain must follow pleasure as day follows night.

But love is different.

Love is not liking. Love is beyond liking and disliking. Love is the point of the pyramid of existence, not part of it.

It is possible to love someone without liking them. As it is possible to like someone without loving them.

Real love is where you neither like nor dislike and yet are not indifferent.

You must no longer confuse love with liking and

disliking.

This will start to happen naturally as you continue to read on and begin to see in the reflection of your daily life how dependent you are on the stimulation of liking and disliking. To see your dependence in the moment it reveals itself is sufficient. No effort or method is required.

When you no longer confuse love with the interaction of liking and disliking, you will no longer be looking for love to excite or stimulate you.

Then you will find love in person, or love will find you, as surely as the sun shines uninterruptedly beyond the earthly illusion of night and day.

Love will come to you without your looking for it.

Suddenly, it will be there.

But at first it may not move you, let alone attract you. For a while you may not even notice it. Why would you, when you have only learned to notice what you like or do not like?

Love is always recognisable by the absence of choice in it.

It comes, it happens and it is happening....and sometimes because you cannot like it or dislike it you cannot believe it is happening......and yet you see it is happening.

You cannot choose love as you would choose a bride or a lover. Love chooses you. And there is no mistake.

When it comes, love will teach you — to be yourself.

But if you are still too deeply attached to liking and disliking, you will see and want some choice in what love brings; you will react from there in the same old way and it will teach you nothing but the lesson the chooser never learns: pleasure always turns to pain.

Love is joy and joy has no opposite.

You may not be able to say you like what love brings. But you will not be able to say you dislike it either. It will be *right* and that will be sufficient for you — until you realise further that love is here, that that which is sufficient to itself, is love.

First, love will teach you how to love yourself.

It will do this by compelling you to give up disliking and liking yourself. You will lose that choice. And you will feel like you are dying.

It will then teach you not to like or dislike where you are. You will lose that choice too. And you will feel that you are dead.

All this will seem like pain, not like love.

But the pain while it lasts will be only your own choosing to hold onto some object or image of love and not love itself.

And in your pain or ignorance you may choose to leave love to have what you like — along with what you do not like — for another round of time.

But always love comes again in the same choiceless way.

Finally, when you are ready, when your likes and dislikes have lost most of their substance, love will provide the choiceless opportunity for you to serve love with your life so that you will never have to choose or want again.

17
THE UNHAPPY SUPERMIND

The world today is run, not by men and women leaders of the various nations who appear to have control, but by the unhappy supermind — the supernormal, super-rational analysing mind.

This is the amazingly clever intelligence of the psychic force of unhappiness that has possessed humanity through the child, through the subconscious — and sustains the possession through humanity's attachment to the past and the individual's unhappiness.

The mental part of the mind controls the thinking side of every single person, as the emotional part controls the feeling side.

The supermind is purely mental and emotional, therefore loveless and lifeless. It is dehumanising — taking the life and love out of — the human race.

The mental part is seated in the memory of

everyone making them think and talk about the past; and the emotional side is seated in the sentiments and attachments of everyone's likes and dislikes, making them live off their feelings of the past.

In yourself, the loveless and lifeless working of the mind is immediately recognisable. The mind can only THINK about love and life. It cannot BE love and life now. So it is distinguished by being unhappy about love and life. Whenever you are unhappy about love and life, that is the mind working.

And the mind while unoccupied must always remain unhappy because it cannot be the absence of unhappiness that is love and life, which you alone can be.

So the mind *thinks* about love and life and *feels* unhappy or gets emotional about both.

This makes it *think* and *feel* that something is missing on earth, or in the world, and that whatever exists has to be changed to try to find what is missing.

So the supermind — in its unhappiness and search for what it can never find because it can never be — moves people and nations around, ceaselessly changing all that exists in the world, without ever getting any closer to love and life.

It is the cleverest and most forceful thing in existence.

But because it can never be the truth, never be love and life, it is utterly ignorant, utterly unhappy, self-perpetuating and ultimately, in its terrible unhappiness, self-destructive.

In its search for what it can never find, the super-rational supermind is taking man and his children every day further away from feeling contact with blessed life on the blessed earth, and the ever-present love within, by seducing him into a sterile electronic (mentalised) existence.

The children are vanishing into imagined worlds of space where there is no blessed life or love at all. And the adults are losing themselves in a lifeless and loveless electro-magnetic dependent world of ultra-clever computerised, mentalised gadgetry — and calling it life.

The women are dying for love but don't know it or they would be able to do something about it.

And the men, seduced and reduced once again by a new eve of technology, are dying for life as they disappear head first into their meaningless inventions and devices.

Man, woman and child are either elated, bored or depressed — depending on which button the mind happens to be pushing or not pushing.

18
THE DEHUMANISING
OF THE LANGUAGE

The super-rational analysing mind — your mind — is the architect of our loveless and material times.

And one of its chief destructive activities is the dehumanising of the human language, all tongues.

This means taking the life — the communication value — out of key words. Key words are words originally formulated by the race to express the beauty and joy of life on earth and within.

Five such words are love, peace, beauty, life and truth.

Each key word represents a state of being.

Originally, when the language was young and vital before the mind in its unhappiness was able to start degrading it, the word evoked in the hearer the actual sensation of the state of being of the person using it. No one used a word that did not represent themselves at that moment.

Language then was not a mental process as it is today. Dictionaries describing the meanings of words would have been impossible.

In fact, words were actually sounds that ran together like wordless songs. The sound alone communicated the sensation. Language was more like birdsong.

With deterioration due to the mind's unhappy activities, mansong — the song of life made conscious — degenerated into wordsong, chanting, mantras and speech.

In our loveless and material times, the method used by the mind to dehumanise the language is in every mind's senseless (feelingless or stateless) repetition of a word. This destroys the true-life feeling that created the word-sound. It leaves behind a purely cerebral or mental function — an empty word, a rational noise signifying next to nothing.

For instance, the mind has rationalised or cerebralised the living feeling, the living daylights, out of the word love.

Normal daily life — your life — from which every child learns by copying, consists of completely meaningless expressions such as: "How are you, love? Thank you, love. I love that. I love my car. I love my cat. I love dancing. I love this dress. I love school. I love teddy bear," and other dubious ones such as, "I love you."

Through the mind's senseless repetitions, the word has lost its conscious connection with the supreme joy of love or life now, in the individual using it.

Today it stands at best for wavering attachments or self-gratifying sentiments — emotions — that are not love at all; or for casual convenience and mutually agreed deception.

With the result that love, the real thing, is suffocated in the individual whose only alternative is to indulge in romantic notions of love, and lustful thoughts of love.

And so the frustrations and unhappiness of living without the reality of love grow and grow.

Having removed the living truth from the word, the senseless mind is then forced to use several additional dehumanised words to try to make up for the word's missing integrity — which of course doesn't work.

So the dictionaries grow fatter, the learned discussions longer and the computer memory banks more necessary. While the truth of life which is vital communication between people, grows less; unhappiness or the mind is served; and insincerity is the smiling practice and posture of the day.

Into the feeling-less mind's senseless rational shredder have gone all the other meaningful words.

And all have come out the other end practically empty ciphers, fit and able to serve only the mind's particularised likes and dislikes and fanciful imagination of what is important.

LIFE, the unpossessable but immediate simple sweetness of being of the earth that is the substance of man's ever-present immortality or true self, is mistaken for living, the dehumanised form of life-without-purpose that is pain and living death.

PEACE, the ceaseless state of man's inner vital life available to all now, is tragically identified with the outer peaceless, normal condition of living in between wars and arguments.

BEAUTY, unnameable but ever present within oneself, is unhappily thought to be in the object outside that decays, dies or passes in time.

And TRUTH — "What is truth?" said Pilate — is disguised in all as the lie that suits today's self-interest.

"How do you do? I am pleased to meet you. Excuse me. Thank you. You are so kind. I am obliged. Good morning. Good night. How are you? Good-bye. Yours sincerely. Dear Ms. Smith. Yours faithfully..."

Every expression describing the beauty and wonder of individual people interacting on the earth, is converted by the rational, loveless, feelingless mind into a dead, habitual and formal exercise.

Not surprisingly many men and women today are not sure what the word love means.

They feel the reality of love within but the word love as it is used and demonstrated by themselves and others in living, is no longer true, no longer adequate to express the sweet intimacy, immediacy and vitality or pure passion for life that they feel.

The word is just too phoney.

And it has even caught on with the senseless masses — the unconscious bionic brain of the loveless mind.

So along with their empty words they give gifts and write nice-sounding sentences consisting of other dehumanised words — all vainly attempting to communicate the one true simple feeling of love or life on earth that is only in the being of love, the being of the word, and not in the utterance or scribing of it.

19
WHAT IS TRUE
IS NOT THE TRUTH

Science, business, industry and technology — the wonders of the age — are the latest expressions of the super-rational mind.

They are not concerned with the truth.

They are concerned only with what is true.

What is true is not the truth.

What is true changes in time according to circumstances.

The truth — love, life, beauty and peace — never changes.

It is true that man has legs. But that is not the truth. Because not all men have legs. Some lose their legs in time. And the contradiction or qualification is then true: man has legs; but that particular man does not have legs.

In the truth, there is no contradiction or qualification.

So science, business, industry, technology and the

information media that publicise their activities, are forced to deal in the particular, whereas what is true keeps changing according to the particular pursuit or liking.

The truth of science, business, industry, technology and the media is that everything worthwhile in life is in the future (or the past) and does not exist now: so it has to be pursued.

Each pursuit is a movement, never an achievement, never an end in itself as the truth is.

And the pursuit of all pursuits is called progress.

Progress is the overall movement or aberration of the rational analysing mind.

As what is worthwhile — love, life, beauty, peace and truth — already is and never changes, any movement or pursuit has to be a movement away from it.

So science, business, industry, technology and the media — representing the great movement of progress — each day take man further and further away from the truth of himself.

They are a movement towards what might be true in the future but which will still change in the particular, making the next movement, the next action, the next aberration absolutely or compulsively and unarguably necessary.

This truthless, ever-restless fixation makes all men the slaves of progress.

And progress is nothing more than the frantic flight from truth and love of the escapist emotions expressed through the loveless and materialistic progressive mind or world.

No movement is possible in truth.

No movement is necessary to find the truth.
There is nowhere to go, nothing to be achieved.
Love, life, beauty, peace and truth are now.

They are you — now — behind the seductive movement or restlessness of your rational progressive mind.

20
THE WORD

Through modern science, business, education, government, industry, technology and the information media, the unhappy supermind is dehumanising — taking the life and love out of — the language and its people at an unprecedented rate.

As a result, the plummeting descent towards total dehumanisation of both — the extinction of life and humanity, or the need of any language or people at all — has never been as blatantly obvious.

Man exists on this planet only to communicate life and love as the truth or being of himself. Once he ceases to do this the justification for his existence ends.

Language is communication and people are communication.

At any time the people of the earth are as real as what they talk about or communicate.

The question at any time is what are they, or what am I, communicating with my life?

As far as "they" are concerned you can get the answer by watching the news tonight.

For yourself the question is: is my life communicating the self-knowledge or joy of life? Or am I communicating some other notion of life or knowledge that I have picked up or learned as my occupation and am ignorantly regarding as the purpose of my life?

The scientist, businessman, official, industrialist, educationalist, technologist or media person cannot communicate love and life because their activities are not concerned with love and life, not concerned with the truth. They are concerned with a degraded knowledge and experience *outside* themselves, both of which are acquired and lead to self-doubt, loneliness, confusion, lack of love and lack of life for themselves and all others influenced by them.

So their activities, like their words, are dehumanising.

Just as the child — or anyone — cannot talk about their likes or dislikes without their unhappiness or unreality talking through them, so no man or woman can communicate the truth or reality of themselves through their occupation: it will always be an expertise or knowledge talking through them that they have acquired and is not themselves — the medium or life they have chosen for avoiding the truth within. What they say or do to serve that occupation will have no love or life in it — no reality.

These people — which is all people — will talk about everything but the truth of life and love within themselves now.

They will talk about a subject outside of what they are now. Their words will refer to the past or future, or the present related to some object or condition, but not to the now that is the wonder of the truth of being life now.

What these learned and knowledgeable people say may be true in some particular, somewhere, or at some other time, but it will not be the truth of you or life now.

So it will sophisticate, complicate and corrupt.

Each time the scientist, official or expert utters or repeats what he (or she) thinks is true, the language he uses is dehumanised, made more lifeless for himself and everyone using it.

And to the degree that the man believes what he is saying is the truth, or identifies himself with it as a way of life, he dehumanises himself — along with all who believe him and even listen to him.

As a result he and everyone else has to find a little more stimulation — good or bad — to feel alive. So life as living becomes ever more complicated, never enough without needing more.

Every moment of every day in the frantic unhappy world the process of dehumanising man and his language goes on gaining momentum.

Nothing but the truth can restrain it.

But there is not enough truth in the world — not enough real individuals, or real words to restrain it.

The truth is only as powerful, as real, as the word, that is, only as powerful as the life of the individual man or woman.

For finally, Man *is* the Word.

This is the ultimate truth of yourself. And it is described in the opening of the New Testament Gospel of John: "In the beginning was the Word and the Word was with God and the Word was God ..... In him (the word) was life .... and the Word was made flesh."

This does not refer to a distant, historical saviour, or other life.

It refers to you — the Man, the life and love, that is your true self now, the man or woman you are — freed of your unhappiness.

And like all saviours, you must first save yourself.

As the original Word, Man or Sound degenerated in time in the mind, so the degeneration, corruption or complication proliferated into innumerable sounds and words called languages, and into myriads of men called the masses.

As living symbols of the truth on earth, man and woman, like living words of the truth, have no other meaning or purpose in being in existence but to express the truth of life as the truth of themselves. Their meaning is their purpose.

The only occupation in living is to find this truth or purpose within.

Consequently, all men and women crave through the darkness and confusion of their occupations chosen for them by the rational mind and its emotions, to find the meaning, the purpose of life — which is simply to be, to express the man or woman they truly are now, freed of the mind and its unhappy occupations.

But the mind will not allow it.

Each day it drains the language (and the people) of more life and truth.

So each day the words (and the people) have to be multiplied in order to represent even less truthfully and more lifelessly, what is true today — because what was true yesterday has already changed and has to be redefined, redescribed and re-reported.

The jargon, ciphers, graphics, illustrations, lists, discussions, meetings, agendas, conferences, talks and useless information posing as news and informed opinion — every bit of it based on someone's likes or dislikes, their unhappiness — pour out in an appalling torrent from the printed pages, the electronic screens, mailboxes, magnetic speakers and multiple banks of barren, senseless brains behind them.

Little does the super-rational mind and its loveless, lifeless emotions realise that this gigantic descending stream is a repeat in a different time and different medium of the deluge that wiped out the ancient world — a modern flood of blind ignorance that is to destroy all that man thought was true, but was not the truth.

Section Two
part two

DYING TO EXISTENCE

21
IN THE BEGINNING...

What is tolerable or not tolerable in today's pushbutton society of the masses, is what suits the self-interest or likes and dislikes of the ruling authority.

At the beginning of time, the ruling authority on earth was the individual man or woman.

There was no emotion in this authority: no past, no likes and dislikes, no unhappiness — no self-interest.

Each individual was responsible for himself or herself in a way that is unimaginable today and in the last section of this book I describe how the individual can now begin to return to that timeless state.

Also, there was no concept of the masses, that is, no notion or fancy of what "would be good" or "would not be good" for others or for oneself, for society or the world.

No good was seen in the future. *The* good, the only good, was seen, realised or known *now* in the individual. And it was known by the absence of unhappiness in himself or herself.

So it was not "a good" that could be given to another or shared with someone who did not have it as we think of good today. That would have been to create another or second "good", a notional or not-existent-now "good".

Everyone was responsible for their own good.

It was an utterly individual and utterly just authority. One simply took responsibility *now* for the good — the absence of unhappiness in oneself — and all that followed was naturally right or good.

As anyone or everyone could do it (and did it), no excuse existed for not doing it.

Consequently, the notion of a massed good, a social good, a family good, or even of a social or external equality, had no meaning. If all are equal in the timeless good within, all are equal in the unfoldment in time or living of the good without — and what happens is then right, and known to be right, leaving no place for doubt or unhappiness.

These first terrestrials were free of unhappiness or emotion because they were not identified with the physical animal body. The physical body is the source of all emotion, all unhappiness.

They were detached from the senses. They *used* the senses to perceive the natural wonder of earthly existence. But they retained the self-knowledge that they were the life, the consciousness, within or behind the body or the senses. And in that self-knowledge they knew that what they perceived through the body — the heavens and the earth — was only a micro-fragment, represented in time, of the timeless universe of life within.

These original terrestrials, being detached from the body although still within it, were individuals.

Individuality vanishes with identification with the body.

Today, man and woman are almost completely identified with, or emotionally attached to, the animal body. This means they accept the body's mortal nature — its justified fear of death and extremely limited vision of life — as their own.

This then forces them to behave according to the rudimentary psychology of the animal or the body. And that creates problems.

The animal body conceals its vulnerability from itself, and finds its comfort and peace of mind in the notion of the masses — in belonging to the herd.

This is natural to the animal instincts of the body, but not to the individual man or woman, the consciousness behind it.

So when the earth was ruled by these people (who are you and I now in a different time) it was not a collective or tribal rule. And it was not a rule by one privileged person, a chief or king.

Each individual ruled — by ruling himself or herself.

There was no place for group responsibility — the misguided attempt to produce a notional second good — which divides and corrupts the rulership of the modern world. Such divisive and disruptive authority would have been utterly irresponsible.

Man and woman's one and only responsibility was to life — to keep unhappiness, the emotion of the fearful herdal animal instinct, out of themselves.

And that required no consultation, no consensus,

no division, no decisions, no tomorrows, no time.

That was done *now*.

Being free from unhappiness, each man and woman was the pure joy of life on earth; and being conscious of that joy as no instinctive animal can be, each was responsible for the joy on earth of *all* life — by simply refusing to have unhappiness or emotion in himself or herself.

For life on earth only suffers from man's unhappiness. When he is joyous within, nothing suffers, including himself.

All life at that time, although outwardly discrete in its myriads of physical forms, was united in man's consciousness or inner sense of responsibility, which was his endless joy of being himself in such a wondrous existence.

He was the timeless consciousness in time — the miracle that is man.

In his beautiful male and female bodies, he was the flower, the fully conscious head of the stem, of all the earth's beautiful instinctive species.

He was indeed sovereign of the earth, the only authority and power required to maintain and preserve the joy of life on it.

Within, as a continuous awareness, he felt and perceived his nature as joy and bliss independent of the physical senses; and yet, when using the senses he felt and perceived his inner joy and bliss reflected in every form of nature on the exquisite earth.

This man was (and is) in paradise on earth.

As all fear and desire for exclusivity arise from the herdal fear of death of the body, man's life on earth was free from fear.

Immortality, along with justice, truth, love, life and the law, were inseparable from the joy and bliss of his nature.

Today's society, organised as a necessity to provide a sort of justice, law or truth outside man, was unthinkable.

In fact, thinking had not been thought of.

As thought — thinking about the past or future — only arises from unhappiness when the natural joy within is missing, man and woman did not think.

Also, as each individual was free within of conflicts and problems, so life on earth without was free of conflict and problems.

As within, so without.

Today, with the whole of society psychically or unhappily possessed and lost in the body consciousness, everyone has a problem or is a problem.

The whole world is a problem — a mass of problems.

And the problem behind it all is choice.

Through their likes and dislikes, everyone's life is spent trying to choose that which will attract what is liked, and that which will keep away what is not liked.

They do not realise what is happening. Their likes and dislikes are purely the assertive reactions of the body's instinctive animal or herdal fears — which are being made self-conscious by the identification of man's superior consciousness with his body.

As the likes and dislikes have become more numerous and subtle in everyone's life, so have the choices, the thinking — and the problems.

This increasing subtlety is regarded by man as

cultural progress.

But really it is the pointless and uncalled for sophistication of the animal instincts in him — their "evolution" or expansion — being forced along by that misplaced identification of his immortal consciousness with the mortal body and its herdal fears or notions.

It was this sophistication that created in him the self-conscious notion of the fear of other herds (other nations) and which led him eventually to develop the Bomb and other genocidal weapons. More recently it engendered in him the contradictory notion of global concern for the safety of the whole herd — humanity, the masses — now endangered by his previous thermo-nuclear precautions.

Today, these two opposing notions of what is good — the survival of humanity or the survival of himself — tear at him relentlessly and divide him and his society.

Since the animal body cannot know the one and only good, it has to continuously chase after countless secondary, notional "goods" — which can never be realised because they exist only in unhappiness.

22

THE EXTRACOSMIC ALIEN

Man's history is the evolution of unhappiness.

It is the evolution of something wholly sinister and wholly alien to life on earth.

This thing does not exist: it is achieving its existence in man individually — through his ignorance or unconsciousness in identifying with the body.

The thing is extracosmic. That is, it is from outside the immediate cosmos that man is involved in.

To the reality of our cosmos it is an inferior parasite.

And yet paradoxically, its existence through man has created the psychic world of life after death.

By creating this psychic world, the alien unhappiness has degraded man's original pristine spiritual state and freedom.

Although there is no death and never was, it has created the unhappy illusion and fear of death and therefore the necessity for its opposite — existence after death.

And now for man to get back to the original pure state of life beyond the existence of unhappiness, he has to repossess this psychic realm — his own subconscious or psyche where unhappiness is lodged.

He must do this by entering his subconscious consciously while alive, and ridding it of the invading parasite. This process starts with the awareness in his own experience of the existence and working of the thing in him.

The extracosmic alien appears in the mind — every mind — as attachment to time.

This in turn manifests as age, as cause and effect, and as the evolutionary and historic principle. Thus, it expresses itself in any logical development linking the past with the present.

The alien is the thinker in man, the reasonable man.

It is time and thought itself.

It is in everything that man can think or feel — apart from his awareness of the natural joy or bliss within that has no object. That awareness is always now, timeless. In that perception alone is he free of it.

The alien is completely false.

It is false because it compels man to believe and reason that the present is dependent on the past, or is the outcome of the past.

It deludes him into thinking and believing that his original timeless state of unending joy, bliss and freedom can only be achieved in time — and not now.

So, imprisoned in this past ignorance, he pursues the impossible — striving through unhappiness to be free of unhappiness and depending on time to be free of time.

Before the alien gained existence in man there was no time, no interval. Everything was and is, now.

Man perceived the beauty or reality of the earth direct through his awareness, now, through the eternal now within him. This means there was no self-consciousness, no self-interest between him and the beautiful earth, no psychic world, that is, no ignorant unhappy subconscious to provide the notion of time, reflection, past or the continuity of existence.

Everything was immediate now, utterly discontinuous, present, ever new.

In other words, the eternal, the timeless consciousness of the earth itself, was immediately present in man's perception, as man's perception.

With no past existence, no psychic subconscious between the earth and the eternal as there is now, there was no evolution.

Evolution, or change, started only when this extracosmic alien force, time — attachment to impressions of the past — entered man's awareness, or his one and only good sense, his perception of the one and only good.

Being intolerable to his timeless consciousness, it was instantly ejected; and formed a subconsciousness — or *the* human subconscious — on top of man's timeless or eternal consciousness.

Before being ejected, the extracosmic force or alien intelligence formed an impression in itself — in time — of man's timeless sense of the one and only good. But as it was only an impression of the good, and not the real thing, it differentiated necessarily into several *secondary* "goods" or secondary senses — which in time appeared as the physical sense organs of hearing, tasting, smelling, touch-feeling and seeing.

This marked the beginning of the evolution of the species (the senses) on earth — their externalisation as a physical world on top of the subconscious.

There was now the eternal consciousness, the subconsciousness and the physical consciousness — the three realms of existence, one on top of the other.

It took immense epochs of unhappiness, of the suffering of all life in time, to finally evolve what we now know as the five different human sense organs fixed in the head as the ears, eyes, nose, palate and skin.

Like stalks, they emerge from the human brain which itself was the product of the same time, past pain and evolutionary trauma that produced all the earth's mortal or sense-perceived creatures.

The earth we know in its familiar shape and form also is an externalisation in time.

It is an externalisation — two levels up — of the pristine terrestrial psyche within, the timeless and changeless — the eternal.

Once externalised through the senses, the earth-image and human psyche entered time or evolution — change.

And immediately, the manifested earth, representing the previously joyous human psyche, re-enacted with cataclysmic violence the agonising effect of the invasion of unhappiness.

The evolutionary evidence of these primordial and subsequent cosmic convulsions and upheavals are preserved today in the dramatic rock formations of the earth's surface. These — its geological history — in truth represent the petrification in stone of the fundamental unhappiness in the human psyche and the existence that came out of it.

The evolution of unhappiness in time continues to be demonstrated in both the human subconscious and the earth.

Just a few miles below the earth's solid crust, the fiery oceans of molten rock — like the endless emotions of unhappiness that still seethe in the tormented human psyche or subconscious — intermittently push and boil to the surface with uncontrollably destructive force.

Nevertheless, for the time being it can be said that the geophysical evolution or manifestation of the earth is "completed" or stable. As is the organic evolution of all the species that culminated in the physical brain and body of man.

Physical earth and physical body are complete.

However, unhappiness on earth is now evolving or externalising in a new medium.

It is manifesting through the unhappy brain as man's emotions — his fears, doubts, violence, cruelty, greed, loneliness, depression, anger and despair.

These emotions all arise from the brain's evolutionary attachment to its animal body and its animal herdal past.

23
THE MASSED UNCONSCIOUSNESS

The multitudinous emotions in man's subconscious, in which he finds comfort excitement and his personal identity, have manifested or externalised as the unhappy unconscious masses of people on the earth.

The masses, like the unhappiness they represent, do not exist.

They are a notion, a reassuring dream of the human brain.

The notion or dream of the masses arises from the brain's evolutionary animal instinct of the herd out of which it emerged.

As the instinctive animal brain finds its safety and identity in the herd, so unhappy evolutionary man hides from the truth of himself in the unconscious activities or dream of the masses.

There he clings to his unhappiness unable to exist until he dies.

In living he never really comes to life; he only thinks he does. He lives, not as an individual, but through the notions of the herd and the herd-instinct.

Only the individual has the power to come to life in existence beyond the herd.

The masses, the herd itself, have no hope.

24
DEMOCRACY: MAN'S LAST UNHAPPY CHOICE

In the modern world the unhappy people's first concerted attempt to make themselves happy was to introduce representative democracy.

Democracy, it was hopefully thought — the masses always live on hope which they do not have — would make everybody happy.

Each man through the democratic vote could express his unhappiness by choosing another emotional or unhappy person or party to express his unhappiness for him to other groups of unhappy parties.

Then these unhappy parties working unhappily together would produce happiness.

That was the hope, the notion.

The vote indeed allowed the unhappy masses to express their unhappiness at the time. But as they did not exist, their vote predictably had no effect. That is, man was no happier; or his unhappiness was no less.

Then just seventy years ago he suddenly discovered that his other sex — his female partner in unhappiness — did not exist democratically (which as he himself did not exist was near the truth). So he gave her unhappiness the vote, too.

Now everyone could express their unhappy choice and everyone would be happy (it was hoped).

But that didn't work either.

Man was still unhappy.

So busy in the meantime were the two sexes working out their unhappy self-interests — he proudly extolling the merits of his democracy to unhappy natives of other lands who like himself did not really exist, and she trying to contribute her unhappiness to the non-existent happiness of democracy — that they both failed to grasp the awful truth of what they had done.

All power comes from the people.

They had willingly handed over for all time to unhappy men outside themselves responsibility for their unhappiness.

It had been a very gradual, creeping transition. But now, with this one seemingly progressive act, the individuality of man and woman disappeared into the ignorance of the masses.

In all of man's thousands of years of trying to cope with unhappiness, he had not done anything so foolish and irresponsible.

Through the ages violent unhappy men had destroyed or seized his possessions, enslaved him and tortured him. Under countless unhappy kings and tyrants he had accepted his unhappy lot as his own, dealing with it in himself as best he could. But never had he voluntarily handed over to other unhappy men, as he had now, the right to make him unhappy.

In fact, throughout his long history he had frequently died to keep that right — that extraordinary inner responsibility or power — rather than surrender it to anyone. He called it his honour and integrity.

That power to him was God.

In that power alone resided his individuality. And only he, the individual, could answer for it or to it: no other.

It was not a notional God or good, as god or good is today.

It was a living state, a being within, the being of himself, the unmistakeable presence of his own rightfulness.

In those earliest of days, life as the feeling of being alive was far more vital in man. He was not a notional, mental creature as he is today living mostly in his head. He possessed far less notional and theoretical information about living and far more knowledge (self-knowledge) of life. He was informed from within.

Over the centuries, however, as he slowly degenerated towards the folly of democracy — the notion that freedom could be attained through others outside himself — he became aware of a growing inner unworthiness battling with his inner rightfulness.

It was like being two opposing living realities at the same time — intensely real as we cannot know it today due to his more conscious state.

Later, after a long interval of further degeneration from consciousness to self-consciousness, man called this inner struggle, his conscience.

But the struggle by then was no longer real. From

a deep vital/spiritual struggle, it had deteriorated into a mental/emotional surface struggle. The struggle of his conscience was little more than a confused contest between various notions of good and bad that others had implanted in him due to his lack of inner knowledge of the one good.

Originally, when the struggle was still a vital/spiritual one, man had the continuous experience of the invading outer force of unhappiness, the mortal in himself, literally grappling like a wrestler with the inner power, the immortal or eternal in himself.

He was simultaneously both of the combatants and frequently did not know, while the battle raged, which would win.

Always he was aware that it was a life-and-death struggle.

It was extremely painful at times, as though he were being killed.

And yet out of that dying, when the power temporarily overwhelmed the force, came the spiritual awareness of the ineffable sweetness and beauty of the life or reality within him — his integrity.

Man lived with death — within him.

Death was a constant presence, an extraordinary energetic activity — not a cessation of it. And when he faced it — alone as he must within — he won the battle, and death brought life! Yet every notion in him of what was good or bad, fought against it!

In this inner death and dying was his saviour and crucifixion.

And so it was, until the priests with their wicked notions entered him as his conscience of good and bad; and in their unhappy worldliness corrupted him into believing that there was a saviour, a crucifixion and a resurrection outside himself.

Living with the presence of death within him enabled man to know the living reality of life within him — honour, integrity, living power, living God, living good.

Honour and integrity are only realised, made real as oneself, in the face of death.

Today, man and woman have little opportunity, and even less inclination, to die for their integrity or honour, the one Good, the one God within.

Today they die for democracy, the god without.

Or they die for some similar mass notion of a good or god outside themselves.

Man and woman choose no longer to live with death within.

It is too painful — and inconvenient.

25
THE DEATH OF GOD:
THE FIRST POPULAR CHOICE

The introduction of democracy marked the end of man's inner fight for life.

He surrendered unconditionally to the notional outer good, the notional outer god, the notional outer existence of the massed unconsciousness. Death — not man — won.

And man gave up the ghost.

The ghost, his false impression of himself, stepped out and attached itself to his new outer body, the notion that he was one of the masses of everybody.

His power and integrity could now only be expressed through force and emotion. He would have to fight for what he thought was right and when he did he would be misunderstood — and would bring more unhappiness upon himself and everybody.

Man had abandoned the reality of himself within the body for a non-existent hope and dream of mass salvation, herdal happiness, outside the body — modern democratic society.

The popular notions and emotions of the massed unconscious now took over.

What was popular was what mattered — not what was right.

The individual's chance of discovering the truth or power within to rid himself of unhappiness was enormously reduced.

Such individuality was not popular.

Individuality was being superseded.

God — the individual within — was dead. And the disease of death spread outwards.

Life on earth was dying.

The more it died the more the masses, the disease itself, lived and multiplied.

And the more the masses lived and multiplied, the more they killed life on earth.

All power comes from the people — as all unhappiness derives from the power the people have surrendered to the force.

26

THE END OF RESPONSIBILITY

The unhappy democratically elected politicians were now responsible for man's unhappiness.

They did the job well. They made man and woman very unhappy.

And unlike at any other time in the evolution of unhappiness on earth, they made man and woman unhappy *indefinitely*. Not even the most wicked kings and tyrants of old had been able to manage that.

The old despots could be murdered, or they simply died. And their inhumanities vanished with them: the King is dead, long live the King for the new King might be compassionate and just.

But democracy did away with individuality.

No single individual was responsible any more with his or her life.

And certainly, no individual was responsible for the injustices and cruelties implicit and endemic in democratic society.

These inhumanities now continued indefinitely.

No more did the murder or death of any person in authority, or even of many persons in authority, make the slightest difference.

Another person or persons, still not responsible, simply stepped in and filled the gap.

Democracy — with its injustices, cruelties and politicians — just went on and on and on and on...

And so did the faceless law-enforcers and law-upholders who were now needed in increasing numbers, or force, to protect the progressively unhappy democratic society from itself. These firm defenders of the arguable, therefore unjust, democratic law, also were not responsible.

Which raised the question that nobody in democracy or in their right mind dared to ask: someone in democracy must be responsible — who?

The people. All power comes from the people. The people must be responsible.

No, not any more. The people handed over responsibility to the politicians.

Then the politicians must be responsible?

Impossible. The politicians are not responsible. Everyone knows that. The politicians don't take responsibility for the poverty, greed, dishonesty, cruelty, exploitation, crookedness and inequality which the democratic system preserves and fosters. A political initiative or individuality strong enough to remove these iniquities might make the people happy — and the politicians' sole responsibility is to make the people unhappy.

Then it has to be the people who are responsible?

It can't be. There are no responsible people any more — where are they? It is not allowed.

Then no one is responsible?

Yes. That is democracy and that is its invincibly popular appeal. Freedom without responsibility is the popular notion of the human herdal instinct.

★

Nevertheless, under democratic rule, man thought he was happier.

That was the popular notion.

Increasing creature comforts and material convenience — the pay-off in someone else's poverty — helped to keep his mind off the personal pain of unhappiness within that just would not go away for long.

The common pay-off, the common weal, the common wealth was shared out no more justly than it ever had been.

The popular notions that justice and happiness had increased were just two more spurious arguments devised by man to try to compensate for loss of contact with his integrity, honour or God within.

If justice and happiness were increasing then everybody must be doing well.

So the unhappy rich (I like) got richer, the unhappy poor (I dislike) got poorer — and the unhappy in-betweens (the masses) multiplied marvellously.

The in-betweens — led by the unhappy politicians and their unhappy political assemblies — maintained their position by mouthfully and emotively defending both the rich and the poor at the same time — and doing absolutely nothing about getting rid of either.

The status quo of unhappiness on earth, like its globally creeping democratic superstructure, was now fixed to the end of time.

And of course man was still unhappy.

But now, with all this distraction going on outside him, he was less aware of the pain of unhappiness within.

And yet, as his awareness of the pain within diminished, so, strangely, did his feeling of being alive.

He was far more knowledgeable in his opinions, had an immense wealth of information in his memory, and knew what was right and wrong for the world.

He also knew he was alive: that was unarguable.

Yet he couldn't feel it.

Which, if you look at it, is what a clever computer or robot might say.

So now, to bolster his failing, feeble feeling of life within, he required more contrived excitement without.

Democracy did not let him down.

All was provided: more alcohol, more fancy food, more entertainment, more television programmes, radios, music, news and information, cars, business, holidays and sexual stimulation through the fantasies of films, magazines, newspapers and the sex shops.

In spite of it, he was still unhappy.

And to add to his unhappiness — which drove him deeper into material escapism to try to forget it — the awful truth gradually dawned on him: never again could he do anything *individually* to stop the politicians or the democratic system from making him unhappy.

No matter how much man tried in his modern

democratic society to publicly protest and demonstrate his unhappiness, there was no one in authority to hear him and do anything lasting about it.

No one was ever responsible enough.

Only what was liked or disliked by the ruling emotional authority — the politicians and their self-interests — got done.

Man's only remaining right of protest, outside of the notion or hope of it, was the ballot box every three or five years. And then his vote only gave some other unhappy person the right to protest for him — perhaps.

Sometimes in his extreme unhappiness he took the law into his own hands.

Acting as an individual he tried to rectify the injustice and inequality of the democratic system, or to force a particular result.

When man is responsible enough as an individual to take the law into his own hands, putting his freedom or life at risk, it is always in an attempt to correct or expose a fundamental wrong in society.

So in an effort to eliminate the gap between the rich and the poor, the privileged and underprivileged, he stole, cheated and otherwise abused his fellows.

And quite rightly, the full force of democracy — the blind or blindfold statute of the democratic law — came down on him like a ton of bricks.

He was beaten, humiliated, sometimes tortured, punished and/or locked up.

The message of the law was clear: he must learn never to interfere with the ineffective democratic processes.

These were designed to perpetuate the unhappiness in the system, NOT to eliminate it.

To eliminate the unhappiness would be to destroy the system.

That would not be tolerated.

The lesson was, he must not act as an individual.

The law was his protection — from himself.

He must remember that for any responsible action he could forfeit his life.

And anyway, responsible action would only cause more unhappiness, more irresponsibility; as he should understand now that he had had a taste of both from the law in being punished for trying to act responsibly.

If he *had* to act responsibly to try to right the injustice and cruelty of the democratic society, he must do it irresponsibly.

That is, he must act in secret, disguise himself, hide himself, deceive and blame others, misrepresent himself and lie so that no one would suspect what he was up to.

He must cheat, rob, exploit, injure, defraud, steal — but never get caught.

The justice of this was that while he could get away with his irresponsible actions, the democratic society would continue to get away with its irresponsible actions. That was quite tolerable, in fact essential.

The democratic law would only ever punish those who got caught.

The lawbreakers were as essential to the society as the law-enforcers. The law, really, was only to allow those two minorities to fight it out and provide a distraction from what was really going on.

For the rest, it was open slather all round: take what you could get away with and call it either healthy competition or socialism.

27
THE ULTIMATE ATROCITY

There is a highly secret, unwritten law behind all the nicely legalised and documented democratic laws.

No one, of course, is responsible for this law. This means that if ever the effect of it on someone is accidentally publicised it can be confidently declared by the highest democratic authority not to exist.

The unwritten law is seldom discovered by anyone outside the would-be individual who breaks it.

The penalty for infringement is democracy's ultimate atrocity and sham.

Here it is:

If a man (or woman) is caught breaking the normal law, he must on no account attempt to expose the underlying injustice or cruelty of the democratic system that drove him to take responsible action by putting his life or freedom on the line.

THAT will not be tolerated.

And if his disclosures of the injustice of the system that motivated him start to be too convincing or worrying for his interrogators, he will be declared insane, secretly if necessary, put away without trial and drugged into submission by the unhappy, faceless medical doctors acting in collusion with the unhappy, faceless law.

No one will be responsible for that, either.

The democratic edict is:

- Man must never forget that he willingly surrendered to the politicians and their self-interests the right to be an individual; and he must live with the consequences of that action until he dies.
- There is no escape in democracy except escapism itself and that is all provided.
- He must understand that he is one of the masses, one of the unconscious herd, and that the law represents the masses, the herd.
- The masses must not be disturbed by any responsible action — ever.
- He must conform to the good and bad that is laid down.
- He must get it through his individual head that it is forbidden for anyone at all to be responsible in a democratic society.
- Only in that way can the human ass of an external irresponsible god — the masses — be protected from having to face up to the unhappiness on earth for which it is responsible.

In democracy only the individual suffers, never

the masses, because the masses don't exist except as a notion of the dreaming individual.

Since democracy eliminates the individual, until only the notion or the dream of the masses itself is left, no one suffers in democracy.

In other words, eliminate the individual, and there is no one left to suffer.

That is the philosophy or truth of the democratic way of life.

It is also the philosophy or truth of communism — and of every dictator and repressive regime.

For in the evolution of unhappiness on earth, which is the history of man, all systems produce the same result — the endless tyranny of unhappiness.

28
THE LICENCE TO FOOL THE PEOPLE... ALL THE TIME

In the democratic way of life man discovered one compensating notion (which was not true or it would have made him happier).

That was that he was now democratically entitled to criticise and blame others for making him unhappy.

This he called freedom of speech.

But really it was a lofty-sounding euphemism for the licence to pass the buck for his unhappiness.

Out of this remarkable notion of freedom arose the quintessence of massed irresponsibility and misrepresentation — the unhappy modern newspaper.

Here at last was the voice of the masses, the defender of non-existent democracy, the mouthpiece of man's irresponsibility to man.

On behalf of the massed unconsciousness, and in exchange for a few pence or cents a day, the newspapers indiscriminately blamed everything and everyone under the sun (except themselves) for man's unhappiness —

without ever mentioning or pausing to perceive the cause of it.

This oversight, naturally, made everyone more unhappy, including the unhappy newspaper people themselves.

For newspapers, like all the media, are people.

So morning, noon and night (and with occasional extras) the news people chorused their unhappiness every day more loudly or more sensationally, representing it as important and meaningful, which of course it was not.

No one believed what the papers said or agreed with it for long because it was never the truth. What was represented changed as often as the date, which usually was reliable.

Even so, the notion of having a daily mouthpiece to bellow the world's unhappiness (without any individual having to take responsibility for the monstrous untruth of it all) gave the masses some inexpensive entertainment along with the further notion that some sort of protest was being made, or perhaps something was being done, or happening.....perhaps.

But nothing continued to be done and nothing continued to happen that was really worth reporting — for conditions all over the earth, representing man's unhappiness, continued to get worse.

Sometimes the politicians in their troughs of unhappiness — and egged on by the inexhaustible wailings of the newspapers — sent the brave young men off to war to be maimed and killed; while the equally brave and unhappy women left behind cheered them on and wept.

And while the politicians beamed on, the newspaper people made heroes of whom they liked with the stroke of a half-true report or headline, and assassinated whomsoever they or their self-interests disliked with the comfortable detached irresponsibility of a firing squad.

God save the Queen. Or the King. But what about the people?

Happily, the people didn't matter because none existed for long, which was why all the unhappy people who survived the wars or who stayed behind, soon forgot those who went and what the wars were supposedly about, anyway.

To our glorious dead.

Who?

Freedom of the press — the licence to avoid the truth every day and to blame everything, including death and war, for the unhappiness of the world — was the new golden god or sacred ass of democracy.

All power comes from the people — as all the forces of unhappiness come from the power the people have surrendered.

So the evolution of unhappiness continued through the individual hiding behind the irresponsibility of the masses, the massed circulations and the ratings.

Things on earth were going along nicely: very unhappily indeed.

★

Freedom of the press was a slogan originally invented by the politicians to fool the people they were supposed to be representing.

Freedom of the press simply meant the unquestionable liberty to publish the likes and dislikes of the ruling emotional authority of the day — which of course was the politicians themselves and their self-interests.

They had cleverly chosen the word "freedom" to imply that what was printed was the truth. (Because of this, the public belief that "if it's in the newspaper it's true" continues to persist despite the contrary experience of most people quoted by newspapers).

The politicians controlled and used the early newspapers through the notional weight of their newly-born democratic authority and assumed public respectability.

When this authority started to wear thin with the press, due to the politicians' obvious duplicity and stupidity, they bribed the newspaper people to keep quiet or to mention them in a good light. (When there's no one to sell the loot to, dishonesty disappears).

This they did by revealing non-attributable secrets and confidences entrusted to them, which made the headlines (and of course created more unhappiness); and by quietly altering, and failing to alter, the legislative statutes to favour the continuance of newspaper irresponsibility without accountability, and give it a creeping kind of legality.

The politicians by then had two faces: one for the public who did not know them; and one for the press who did. This led to the further deceit of reporting to newsmen "off the record", or speaking behind the public's back.

The great modern conspiracy had now begun.

Previously, the conspirators had been the rulers and church against the people. Now it was government and press against the people.

With the connivance of the newspapers, and their own public posturings of being responsible, the politicians of democracy were able to institutionalise their most brilliant lie: the notion of the public interest.

By claiming what they liked or disliked to be in the public interest, both the newspapers and legislators were free to protect and further their own narrow self-interests in the name of this broadest and most acceptable notion of the good of all.

However, as the only public interest is for the individual to be rid of unhappiness, any "other" public interest has to be purely emotional, subjective — non-existent.

Institutionalising this brilliant fiction was the consummate cover-up and camouflage, the ultimate in subterfuge and skulduggery.

But between them, the two conspirators managed it.

Which meant that everything the politicians and press now did and said was done and said "in the public interest". If this couldn't be proved, it couldn't be disproved: it was a matter of opinion or endless debate.

And as only the media and politicians possessed the means to broadcast their opinions, their likes and dislikes, and to debate what they liked or didn't like, all was well.

The public interest was being served.

And yet, historically, the notion of the public interest was no more of a wicked fabrication than that institutionalised by the priests, the previous co-

conspirators against the people.

The priests, in order to gain emotional control of the masses and to cause them greater ignorance and unhappiness, had institutionalised the tragically misleading notion that a saviour, a crucifixion or a resurrection — the one good or God — could exist outside the individual now or have any verity in the past; and that some creed, belief, priest or historical book was needed to find it.

Over the millennia, the emotional authority of the priests and church — being based on falsehood — had lost its force to trick and delude the new generations of man. A new form of force was now needed to dupe him again, and to allow history, or the evolution of unhappiness on earth, to continue to repeat itself.

For all unhappiness lies in repetition.

The politicians, by selling their souls to the media, provided it.

The ghost of unhappiness that had passed from man to the politicians, now stepped out of the body politic, into the sensational body of the media people — the unhappiest of all the unhappy masses on earth.

Like the man and woman before them who had surrendered their individuality to the notion of democracy, the politicians were not to realise until later what they had done, and what their dishonesty and chicanery had unleashed upon the world.

Nothing was to have such awful consequences for the masses and the earth as this.

The media owners and their journalists, without any authority from the people —which at least the tricky politicians had had — seized the democratic right to speak directly for the unhappy masses; and at the same time to decide what the masses should be told and should not be told each day.

It was an outrageous usurpation of supposed democratic right by an utterly irresponsible section of unhappy people trained in the habit of distortion to make man and themselves more unhappy by presenting the untruth as the truth.

Nothing makes man more unhappy than this.

For murder, opinions, robbery, war, vanity, greed, corruption, problems, death, violence, scandal, slavery, illness and grief on which the media people thrive are the effects of unhappiness, not the cause.

To report, investigate, discuss and expose them day in and day out is as unreal and meaningless as saying in endless different ways that water is wet.

Water *is* wet. And existence *is* unhappiness.

The only intelligent question is, why is water wet, and why is existence unhappiness?

Since it is an intelligent question there is no answer — only the solution.

Water is wet only when you go into it or it goes into you. Wetness is an effect.

Wetness is not water. Water, in fact, is life.

In the same way, existence is only unhappiness when you lose yourself in it, believe in or serve its unhappy effect; or if you allow its unhappiness, its effects, to enter you. Existence, in fact, is bliss.

The only news that is new and real is the news of the cause of unhappiness and how to be rid of it.

That alone is the truth.

When a person's full-time occupation is presenting the untruth as the truth to the people — misrepresenting the effects as the cause — the unhappiness engendered in the person is prodigious.

In the young journalist and TV reporter the excitement or liking of such power-without-responsibility — the herdal utopia that is not given to many people on earth — manifests as an almost frantic enthusiasm, a blind dedication to the propagation of the untruth as the truth.

But in the maturity of time or age, the unhappiness ossifies into a chronic world-weariness, a sterile scepticism that comes from having seen all the effects — but not the cause.

Frequently alcohol, the dry outer spirit, provides the only relief; and finally, for many, the only escape.

Two things made the media takeover possible:

- the funk and greed of the politicians
- and the shameful deception the politicians had knowingly initiated and legitimised as freedom of the press, hiding behind the equally fictitious notion of the public interest.

"Freedom of the press in the public interest" had been repeated and jingo-ised often enough for the hopeless masses to believe it, and for the politicians now dependent on the lie of it, to have to publicly and constitutionally support it.

The way was now clear for the new god of the world — the blind force of unhappiness behind the power of the press — to do what it wanted.

It was to be a slow and subtle process so that no one involved would perceive where it was all leading — for the massed unconsciousness on no account must be disturbed.

The media people themselves had not the slightest inkling. They were too irresponsible, cocksure of their superficial "good story" role, to comprehend its appalling profundity in another time.

They knew the feeling of being in charge — like a child might know it is at the controls of a great airliner while the captain, crew and parents look on applaudingly. But like the child they could not comprehend the overall significance or the responsibility of such power and position, the intelligence of which must know what it is doing and where it is going.

29

THE TERRIBLE PRICE

For their infamy in selling out the people to the press the politicians had a terrible price to pay.

Until the end of time they would be persecuted — rightfully or wrongfully, it was irrelevant — by their new masters, the irresponsible and uncontrollable media, the new ruling emotional authority of the world.

The self-interests of the newspapers, television, magazines and radio stations were now paramount.

Never again would the media owners and their journalists allow the politicians any rest — except the politicians who compromised or did nothing.

Every day, in every democracy in the world, any politician proposing to do some good by eliminating any of the fundamental evils of the democratic society, would be privately hounded and publicly crucified until he sold his soul again for the media — or quit.

The media people never knew where they were

going or what they were doing.

So they did not know where they were leading.

Towards the end, some of the politicians, still tricky but intuitively closer to the good of the people, glimpsed the truth of what was happening. But they were powerless to speak out.

For there was only the media to speak through.

And you can't ask the burglar to fetch the police.

The lie of the public was now complete.

Like the public interest, public opinion was now the opinion of the few unhappy people who reported and handled the news, and the even fewer unhappy people who owned or controlled the means of disseminating it.

And public concern was whatever these few people chose to focus their capricious attention on and inflate as being important.

Democracy was now the media.

But of course not one person in the media was responsible or accountable.

Every action, comment or report was either in the public interest or debatable before the equally irresponsible and unaccountable men and women of the arguable, and therefore unjust, democratic law.

Once it had been rule by man, the individual. Then it was rule by kings and despots; then by democratic politicians. Now it was rule by newspapers, television, radio and magazines.

The politicians always knew what they were doing.

They were crooked and cowardly or opportunistic and hyprocritical but they knew their shortcomings.

Many politicians knew there was a greater good somewhere. But none would die to find it in themselves.

So they settled for a secondary good. And that forced them to compromise with someone else's notion of good and someone else's, and someone else's... Until what they did, by the time they were able to do it, was hardly any good at all.

And they knew that too.

That was doing their best in the circumstances, another compromise.

The media people, however, never knew what they were doing.

They were blind ignorance devoted to being blind and ignorant.

For them the good was in what they were doing: they were serving the truth; they were serving the people. They believed in themselves. So they never questioned themselves or what they were doing.

There is no greater ignorance than that, no greater irresponsibility.

So along with fooling with masses, the media fooled themselves — right to the end.

30
THE ARMY

Sometimes in the evolution of unhappiness on earth the army stepped in and snatched the right to rule from the unhappy politicians and the raving media.

All were shut up or shut down.

And for a while there was no unhappiness to speak of.

This of course made everyone very unhappy indeed, including the army whose strength lies in never having to pretend to take responsibility for anything.

The army is force itself, the force of arms, the ultimate physical violence of the massed herdal unconsciousness.

So far is it from the truth that it is actually closest to representing the truth: life or death now, no time, no considerations, no problems, nothing in between.

When the army tries to take responsibility for anything but force, it becomes political, devious, loses its strength and way, and destroys itself.

The army — the force — must at all times obey the power.

When there is no power other than itself, which is inevitable when it seizes power, it becomes corrupt, political and unjust. Out of that degeneration arises the people's notion of democracy or herdal freedom; and out of that the faithless politicians and the irresponsible media — the full circle.

Pure force is neither just nor unjust.

Force is force.

Force must be obeyed or the penalty is death.

There is nothing in between pure force and death — only instant obedience to the force.

Either you obey or you die.

There is no choice, no complication, no emotion.

That is the army. That is the virtue of pure force. You know exactly where you stand.

The army loses its pure force, its real strength, when it takes prisoners, is burdened with considerations.

Pure force does not take prisoners, has no consideration.

Prisoners — like peace — make the army emotional, unsure of itself, unsure of what to do next.

Prisoners — like peace — make the army have to consider or pretend to be responsible. As its strength lies in not being responsible for anything but forcing immediate obedience or death — once that obedience is implicit in numbers of prisoners or victory, the army has nothing to do, and its pure force is spent.

Then comes the power of the people again.

The unhappy prisoners are absorbed into

the people.

The people in their unhappiness hand over the power to the unhappy politicians and become the helpless masses.

The army is then the unhappy prisoner of the corrupt force or self-interested considerations of the politicians.

Until once again the army seizes the power in peace or war and for a time becomes the pure force: no prisoners, no prisons, no compromise, no considerations, no discussions, no escape — just instant unconditional surrender, obedience or death.

For a while.

The army can never pause to realise that force, itself, is the essence of unhappiness.

If it did, force would change to power.

And the people in the army would lay down their arms and say, "We solve nothing".

And the people in politics would lay down their promises and protestations and say, "We can do nothing".

And the media people would lay down their lies of freedom and twisted view of life on earth and say, "We have nothing more to say till we can say the truth".

Then, the force of unhappiness, the lonely god outside man, would have to step back into him.

And for a short time it would give him hell — but only until he regained the power over it to be himself, to be once more responsible, accountable with his life, for the joy of life on earth.

But as it is in the massed dream of existence, when the army is not in charge, the media through the politicians will be.

And together, each in their cycle, will give man hell till the end of time.

31
BEGINNING OF THE END

With modern communications intensifying the spread of unhappiness around the earth it was only a matter of time before the democratic media people — the unhappiest of all the masses — took over the direction of the world.

Naturally, under such increasingly unhappy guidance reflecting the incestuous in-breeding of the likes and dislikes of a micro-minority, the news of the world got worse and worse and worse....like tonight's news, for instance.

Calamity and disaster were all the beautiful earth and its people were about when perceived through an unhappy eye for profit and advantage, and a nose for news based on the ignorance of life.

Occasionally, the news was presented as a happy (I like) event.

But this too was doomed to turn into unhappiness because the happy person or thing always died or passed away, anyway — an impermanence the media people made sure not to mention or note. Death, like the truth, was unmentionable except as a tragedy because nobody in charge liked it and everybody in charge disliked it. Which sort of got rid of it, sort of.

Practically nothing about the world did man now know except what the media minority chose to tell him.

There were many signs of what was coming.

This book is being written in mid-1985. The story now ranges into the future.

Anyone seriously endeavouring to rid themselves of unhappiness will to that extent be able to discern the truth or otherwise of what is being written from actual events as they develop.

Some of the signs will be extremely subtle. Others will be grotesquely obvious.

But to the person of the unconscious masses nothing very unusual will be noticed until the final panic starts to set in.

Even then the causes will not be seen and those culpable will never know what they did — for still no one will be responsible.

One current sign that something has gone cosmically wrong on the planet lies in the proliferating systems of space satellites orbiting the earth. Twenty-four hours a day they are providing instantaneous global communication — of information, but of no knowledge of any value.

These systems should be beaming the good news, the knowledge or terrestrial truth, to boundless life throughout the cosmos that all on planet earth is well and on time and "come on in".

But all is not well. All that is transmitted by the

satellites — symbolising man's finest technological achievements — are two lifeless forms of information: entertainment and bad news.

Entertainment is pleasure — what I like. And bad news when it gets close enough to home is pain — what I dislike.

The ceaseless interaction of these polarities of unhappiness are now intensifying enormously. Man's finest technical achievements, pouring out in a mind-boggling stream that no one person can any longer appreciate let alone catalogue, are a product of man's unhappiness and so in spite of his best intentions will cause more and more unhappiness and discontent.

The worst, like the best in electronics and invention, is always yet to come.

But time is no longer a protection or a barrier.

Any day is the next day of the final breakthrough.

Things can only get worse, not one iota better.

Coming to all nations on a scale not before experienced, nor imagined possible, is civil strife, economic disruption, political instability, morale-destroying assassinations and public murder, terrorist mayhem, massive breakdowns in democratic law and order, riots and war-like destruction of property and security along with open police violence, reprisals and savage army intervention against the democratic masses.

As a lead up to this, the news on home television screens will show increasingly unprecedented police, army and official para-military brutality against the civilian population in the name of maintaining law and order.

These film-reports will be designed — unconsciously, because the media does not know what it is doing — to accustom and harden the viewing public to unparalleled actions of violence yet to come against the people.

In other words, the public are being surreptitiously prepared and educated to accept outrageous demonstrations of cruelty and intimidation by the democratic authorities against themselves as normal, necessary and commendable.

If I am wrong and foolish this will not happen, and is not happening. But do keep watching the television screens — without becoming inured or excusing what you see.

The above civil disturbances in all countries will continue increasing against a background of mounting international distrust often appearing as encouraging co-operation, menacing alignments and fears for national survival. The politicians of all nations will parley and announce hope-raising agreements — but unabatedly the rot will go on, fed and nurtured by the naive media.

The democratic media, now being able to cast around the whole world instantaneously for problems and unhappiness, will seem to run into a goldmine of both.

Never before — and this is today while you are reading this — will there be such a diversity of unhappiness to report.

Significantly, wherever the media reporters go in the world, conditions and unhappiness there will get worse. But no one will notice this sufficiently to mention it and to make any difference. For everyone will think that it is the events making the news. But it will be the news making the events.

At first, particular events will not last long in the headlines because something more depressingly sensational, more stimulatingly bad or lyingly exciting, will keep coming in from the tirelessly unhappy reporters and their masters. Instant eyewitnesses, instant experts, instant seriousness, instant laughter, instant emotion, instant charity, instant everything but the truth behind it all will pour out as news.

To the television viewers, multiplying throughout the world at about the same rate as the bad news, it will be an almost endless treat of human misery and wantonness — a grand entertainment feast like a good seat at the Coliseum on a Lions-and-Christians day.

Ironically, the bad news put out by the communicators of the media will increase in exact proportion to the entertainment they put out. One will balance the other so that the significance of either — or what is really happening — will not be noticeable.

Also, the coverage of both bad news and entertainment will slowly reduce in focus. You will have to watch this happen in the context of future events and technological advances to see what I am saying. As the focus reduces the effect will intensify. This will raise the emotional ambience of the masses.

For a time, the rivetingly exciting (for everyone) bad news (for someone) will seem to be occurring as different happenings in different places around the globe; as the entertainment will be coming from various hook-ups around the world.

Finally, just before the end, the two focuses of entertainment (what I like) and bad news (what I dislike) will merge. The excitement of the bad news will become the main entertainment: no one will want to see or hear anything else.

All the seemingly isolated bad news will now come together into a meaningful whole. And so will the entertainment.

The pleasure will then become the pain, and the pain the pleasure.

Liking and disliking will start to lose their meaning, their value.

Unbridled excitement — panic — will not be far away.

And still no one will realise the simple truth of what is happening and how it is being done although many will sense the approach of something unprecedented in human history.

The simple truth is that the world only exists to give you what you want: the truth, or untruth, whichever you are looking for.

If you are looking for the untruth — or towards the untruth as a way of life — which is what the world's reporters, experts, viewers and readers are doing, you will find it.

The more frequently, vigorously and determinedly you look, the more of it you will find — and more quickly.

So you will become unhappier. Which is precisely what is happening to the world.

Only the approach of the end of time, the end of the age, allows the individual to see this and rid himself of time, the unhappiness of the race. Time at such a time is intensified and reflects its own destruction in timelessness or lack of unhappiness in the individual.

If the reporters and viewers had had enough of the excitement of unhappiness which they are so avidly pursuing and finding so plentifully in the world and in their personal lives, they would start looking for the truth. As the world must give you what you want, events would then reflect that good news in their own lives, in the world and on the television screens.

And they and the world would become happier.

But as it is, the unhappy media people, the viewers and the readers between them, make the bad news.

So every day as they all get unhappier the news gets worse.

Or as the news gets worse they all get unhappier.

32
THE END OF TIME

With the media people now the ruling authority in charge of the emotions of the push-button world, there was no stopping them nor way of preventing the consequences of their ignorance.

The future was theirs.

Since the world only exists to provide what is wanted — the untruth or the truth — the media, like the politicians before them, had to get what they were looking for.

In their extremes of unhappiness and their frantic day and night search for it, the media people would produce the most sensational story of all time — the end of the evolution of unhappiness on earth, the end of the world itself.

And, of course, once again not one of them would be responsible.

Not one of the media people (if any survived) would even know what they had done. Just as at this moment while you are reading this page they do not know what they are doing now and where it is leading.

Unconsciousness cannot realise that it is responsible. Keep watching the media and see the truth for yourself as the world is driven towards the main stream of the final crisis.

So uncontrollable would the newspaper and television people become in their irresponsibility and unhappiness, that eventually they would succeed in disturbing the masses, the massed unconsciousness.

With their lies, distortions, half-true reports and speculations the media people would inflame the global masses into an emotional frenzy of fear and excitement.

Once stoked up with sufficient fear and expectation by the media, the massed frenzy would become self-generating and start a fission reaction.

All power is in the people and the atom, and all force comes out of the power the people and the atom have surrendered.

The massed excitement would now drive the media into unbelievable hysteria (even by today's standards). The media insanity would engulf the politicians. Madness would start to consume the whole global society, East and West, providing the waiting army with the excuse for the final fling of force, the final solution.

In the build-up everyone would again think that it was the news producing the media reports. But it would be the reporting and presentation making the news.

The actual events in the world, and emotions in the masses, would always lag behind the latest exciting lies in the reporting of the events. Until the reporting triggered the final emotions that would create the final explosive event, or the last news.

In disturbing the masses, the media people would awaken the sleeping giant of unhappiness itself.

This is the most dangerous thing in the world. For the massed unconsciousness must never be disturbed. This was something the tricky, but intuitively wise politicians always knew not to do, unless the massive emotions released could be pointed away from home towards a distant enemy. The world wars had been waged and won in this way.

The masses represent the fundamental unconsciousness of matter, the atom itself in which the power of creation or the annihilating force of ignorance is concealed. Once that inertness, that basic unconscious stability is penetrated, shattered, a catastrophic force is released.

This time however there would be no distance separating the masses, no "far-away" enemy. The ruling emotional authority — the media — had made up a global society. The communication of nuclear missiles as the latest news would be instantaneous. There was no space any more between home and the enemy. Humanity was now its own enemy. There was nowhere to go. Home or wherever you were was the battlefield.

The final disintegrating release of force would be accompanied by unprecedented natural disasters.

The earth, representing the human psyche, would repeat the primordial convulsions that had followed the original invasion of unhappiness, or the psyche's conception of unhappiness, at the beginning of time.

Now, however, the natural terrestrial upheavals would represent the death throes of unhappiness at the end of time.

And all unhappiness would disappear with the masses from the face of the earth.

But as the masses and the changing face of the earth did not exist anyway, and as the whole history and evolution of the world was only a dream of the dreamer lost in a notion of a good outside himself, it did not matter.

Only the dream was shattered.

The dreamer was untouched.

And freed of time, freed of the notion of unhappiness, the dreamer, the individual, would wake up to the reality of timeless life on the blessed planet earth within himself, that by the grace of almighty God was still the same as when he dropped off into unconsciousness and left it to build an unhappy world and existence of his own.

Thank God, it was only a nightmare.

He would not drop off again ...... for a while.

Section Three

THE LAW OF LIFE (KARMA)

An Esoteric Teaching
For Those Who Would Be True

Unless you are prepared to be more responsible for your life than most of the earth's population, it may be unwise for you to read further.

Either it will be meaningless to you, or your life will start to change, for better or for worse.

The change, if not for better, should only be temporary. But you will know why it has happened and how to correct it — which is more than most people ever know or learn.

I am going to be telling you about the mystery of life or the secret of living — which then will be neither a secret nor a mystery to you. The price of such knowledge, such real knowledge, is responsibility.

The point is, that whatever happens in your life after you read what I'm going to say, it will be you who is responsible for it, not Barry Long, not this book or any other person or event outside yourself.

Why, will be clearly stated.

But by then it will be too late to change your mind. You won't be able to back out, to go back to where you are now. You won't be quite the same person again. You will already be more responsible for your life than ever before.

You will know what living is about. You will understand what you have to do. You will know how to do it. And you will know what to expect and whom to blame if you don't.

Section Three
part one

DYING FOR LIFE

33
BEING TRUE

Are you being true in your life?

Really being true? To yourself?

Are you living with someone who makes you unhappy? Are you keeping someone who uses you and doesn't love you?

Do you dislike or hate your job? Do you long for love but are no longer vulnerable to love because you're frightened of being hurt? Do you ache to be free?

Are you living with a partner you don't love and making the best of it for the sake of comfort, convenience or the children? Are you putting up with whatever is depressing your joy of life because you're afraid or scared of change?

If the answer is yes to any of those questions, you are not being true. You're not being true to yourself, to life. And even if things do change you won't be happy for long.

Everyone is trying to be true in their way — true to somebody, an idea of something. And it doesn't work. All it does is lead you to not being true to yourself. And that is unhappiness.

Why doesn't it work? Why can't it work?

Because it's impossible to be true to anyone or anything until you are true to yourself.

Then you are true to everyone and all things. And your problems begin to disappear.

Isn't that the most extraordinary thing you've ever had put to you as a practical possibility? I'll repeat it. When you are true to yourself the problems in your life start to vanish.

To be true you have to discover and start to live under the law of life, sometimes called the law of karma.

The world knows very little about this law and understands it less.

The reason is that it's a conscious law, THE conscious law, in fact the one and only real law. It governs full-time the lives of the relatively few conscious, responsible individuals on the planet. And it is available at any time to help those who are prepared and already endeavouring to become more conscious and responsible in their lives.

The karmic law is practically unknown in the world because it applies or functions only in the present, now, without reference to the past.

The world's laws, on the other hand, are unconscious laws, and so are all the moral codes and commandments that men and women impose on themselves and each other or try to live by.

Such unconscious laws are laws founded on the past — past experience. They depend wholly on evidence or rules of the past to establish who is guilty or not guilty in the present.

As it is impossible for anything in the past to be true in the present, unconscious laws are only relatively true, approximately true — and they result in compromise. Compromise is trying to make the best of things in the present circumstances. The effect of these laws is to cause conflict in the person — at best the conflict of conscience — and, in the world, division and discord which we see all around us.

Such unconscious laws arise from unconscious thinking.

Unconscious thinking is thinking based on good and bad and right and wrong. Good and bad or right and wrong are the world's two fundamental unconscious notions. Almost without exception, unconscious laws and beliefs govern the lives of the entire population of the earth, the five billion persons who independently and collectively demonstrate by their daily lives that they are not yet able to be responsible for their destiny as the people of this planet, or for themselves.

If you are unhappy with your life you are avoiding responsibility for it. You are unconscious. You are obligated or considering something or someone and are not being true to yourself, to life.

To wake up and come alive you have to throw yourself on the law of life. You have to refuse to compromise any longer with what is making you unhappy. You have to quit or separate or break with the past. You have to take action.

The action itself may well change the situation or the other person and end the compromise so that you can be new in yourself and continue where you are. But you must break with the old — and not allow it to bind you and blind you again.

If you are hanging on to a situation for the sake of someone else you are deceiving yourself and achieving nothing. When you are unhappy you are not yourself and when you are not yourself you are no real good to anyone — your job, your partner or your child. You will infect them all with your unhappiness, your discontent, and they will suffer or not be themselves. You may think it doesn't show and that you are getting away with it, martyring yourself. But the fact is you are being dishonest and that sort of dishonesty doesn't rob, doesn't steal: it just spoils what should be good.

When you feel compelled to consider another and think you're being unselfish you are merely considering yourself: you consider the person as an extension of yourself and you do them a disservice because they are not that. If you love them you do not have to consider them. You only consider what you do not love. A mother who loves her child does not consider it. Her love knows what the child needs and she acts from there.

If breaking with someone or something makes you think it will be hard on the child you are taking with you, or have to support, you are mistaken. It may be hard on you for a while, making do for you both in the world. But as long as you love the child and share your life with it in love, the child will be happy. You will be happy together.

You are happy in any circumstances with the one you love who loves you. You will manage. You will get through by making the new life an adventure together. If you are being true, and not self-indulgent, vindictive or resentful, the child will understand and enjoy playing its part. But above all, you will be free of the old deadening grip of compromise in your life — and you will be ready for the new.

The new always comes. The law of life will be true to you if you are true to yourself.

Sometimes, to be true to yourself is to stay put where you are. But to be true in such a case — consciously true — means you can no longer be miserable as you used to be. Either you will be surrendered to the situation because it can't be changed (surrender is the conscious acceptance of what can't be changed at this moment but may be changeable in the next) or you will be working consciously full-time to make the situation right. Either way, you won't complain, doubt or become depressed because you'll know what you are doing. You'll be responsible.

When you do break with a person or situation, money can be scarce. But that will be looked after. You'll get through. Have you ever known a time when you didn't get through? Everyone gets through. Everyone has some money. All you need in the first instance is food, warmth and shelter.

Get your priorities right: don't want more than you can have now. Use what you have, what is provided. You are not going to stay where you are. You are getting free. You're not free yet. You're in the process. It is moving every day. Don't look anxiously ahead. Don't be afraid. Life will look after you then, if you are true now. Now is what is important. But do what you know you must. Don't lay about. Be alert. Stay as conscious as you can.

Life can't suddenly provide everything at once. It was you who strangled it while you compromised.

157

Enough for now is enough. Trust in life. It knows what you need. And as you stick at being true, life will provide what you need more and more.

Watch life work. Watch the miracle unfold in front of you as a letter of opportunity is slipped through the door, your eye is drawn to just the right advertisement, or someone makes a casual suggestion that opens up a whole new prospect for you.

Don't fall back into old patterns. Don't get stuck again in the same situation. Be vulnerable, but only to love and to what you know is right in the moment — nothing else. Learn from being true to yourself how to tell the difference.

Don't blame. Don't accuse. Don't tell your sad story. Complain as little as you can. Be new. This is a fresh start. If you acknowledge the old by talking about it you carry it with you. Don't think about it, either. It's gone, finished. And if it turns up again in the form of a person or some other reminder, don't go along with the old emotion it excites. Pause. Hold to your newness. Be true to yourself. The world will always be trying to drag you down, to drag you backwards, and its most powerful weapon is the past.

Don't try to please anyone — mother, father, family, friends. Be true. Don't give in to the tears and emotional demands of others. Yield only to love. Love does not demand — except inside yourself where it demands that you be true to the new state, the new you.

And in those times when you seem to lose that state and clarity, don't despair, don't be discouraged. Don't doubt or think it was all imagination. Hold the pain, the isolation, the confusion, the depression. Be the pain. Don't let it out. Feel your strength underneath.

Don't think. Wait. Be patient.

Resist trying to work out anything in the past. There's nothing to work out. You've done it; or it's happened. You've worked it out by taking action. Let it be.

Don't analyse. Don't feel sorry for yourself. Don't look back. And don't feel sorry for others — that's backtracking. Leave it to life. Be as still as you can. The disturbance and darkness will pass. The lightness and rightness will come again.

Just hold. Be true. You are not suppressing: you are dissolving the problem. It is the law of life in you dealing with the weight of the past in you, reducing the old you, the old problem. You've done what you had to do by quitting, separating or breaking with the past. You did it to bring life back into your life. The pain you feel is only the past dying, not the present. Life — the present, the new — will not let you down.

34
LIVING UNDER THE LAW

Let me say what happens when you do what I have just described, that is, when you are brave and real enough to break with compromise and *consciously* throw yourself onto the law of life.

You call for justice. Real justice.

You exert your sacred right as a human being to appeal *direct* to life for immediate justice. This is a right man has forgotten he possesses.

You *ask* to be judged immediately, now — not as to whether you are guilty or not guilty as the world will certainly judge you, but whether you are being true to yourself, true to life, in what you are doing. By your conscious action you ask *direct* for life's assistance.

To avoid such directness and honesty in their lives, the unconscious masses have invented the *indirect* ritual of praying for help. These prayers use words, thoughts and emotions as substitutes for the direct action of self-sacrifice by which you end compromise, and rid yourself and life of unhappiness.

The action of putting yourself, your life, on the line, is faith. But this is not the popular faith of belief or supplicatory prayer. It is the faith that moves mountains — the kind of mountain of difficulties that seems to loom over you when you break with compromise.

Remember, you *are* life. That life in you is meant to be free. And because you are being true to life, consciously taking responsibility for its happiness, you have nothing to fear. The mountain is only your fears.

The law of life or karmic law is not about penalties. It does not hand out punishments or exemplary deterrents. It is there for the truth — for man and woman who would be true. And like the truth, its justice is extremely simple: at the man's or woman's own direct request it provides the worldly circumstances appropriate to freeing him or her from the injustice of the situation.

So, in such a crisis as I have described in which you remain conscious of the law of life, the circumstances you need to help you in the world, and to help you to remain being true, will occur. Problems will gradually or even instantly diminish.

But if you are not true and invoke the law — meaning, if you just want change, excitement, or to gain something other than freedom from the misery of not being true to yourself — you will attract circumstances that *make* you miserable — to enable you to be more true. In other words, there will be more problems than there are now, or those you have now will last longer or get worse.

Understand that you don't have to be true in the

world — only true in yourself.

One is not the other; but the inner controls the outer.

The whole world of persons of which you and I are parts is robbing, deceiving, exploiting and misleading each other under the guise of commerce, government, society, caring and respectability — and yet every individual inside themselves yearns to give.

No one can be honest in the world for long because everyone in the world is forced to be dishonest: all are compelled to compromise — to make a deal for personal comfort or security with someone or something.

You can only finally be honest, true and uncompromising with yourself. That alone, that inner consciousness, will change the world.

★

To be fully conscious and responsible for oneself is every human being's right and destiny. It means being consciously and voluntarily answerable to the karmic law every moment of your life; and living the law as your own self-knowledge.

Such individuals do not try to hide from the law or ignore it when that would suit their apparent advantage. Any transgressions, they know, will have to be paid for and they willingly watch and accept life's adjudication in order that they may know themselves better, be more true to life — and be more free.

These men and women live and act out of the knowledge that this law is the supreme justice — the justice of being made to be oneself by oneself.

Consequently — and this will be your experience

every time you are true — there is no feeling of being imposed on or alienated as occurs with the world's laws; no feeling of coercion or inferiority. This justice resides in one's own will; it is one's own law, one's own integrity, one's own self. Such men and women are not only conscious but responsible — conscious of life and responsible for it. Compromise and conflict disappear from their being. And in the otherwise divided external world, the circumstances of their lives work together to serve their destiny or life-purpose.

On the other hand, to be unconscious is to be oblivious or ignorant of the presence and power of this law, as most of humanity is.

Such unconscious persons are unavoidably irresponsible to the whole and in conflict with their own being. They live in a divided world of shifting values and colliding circumstances. They have no control over their destiny and no discovered life-purpose.

For such unevolved people, to have to live under the simple summary justice of the karmic law and to have to face knowingly the circumstances of their daily life as reflecting their own inner state of truth, would be a terrifying and unjustly cruel imposition.

So the eternal justice or wisdom itself protects the world and the great bulk of its population from direct knowledge of the law. The protection lies in their combined ignorance: they know nothing about the law, nor do they desire to know. They can't perceive it for themselves and if it is explained to them they can't hear it, or they ridicule it.

In short, it does not exist for them. In their ignorance they are innocent before the law; but because of that ignorance are unable to be freed by it.

Furthermore, they are shielded from the law's devastating implication which I am now going to reveal to you. This, to the ignorant and unconscious people of the world, is the unbearable truth — and for everyone it is the most difficult thing in life to have to face up to. Here it is:

"I, the individual man or woman, am responsible for all the circumstances of my life. As I am within, so is my life. If my circumstances are painful, I am doing it. No one is to blame but I.

So long as I continue to pursue a divided existence, independent or ignorant of the law of life, I will feel incomplete, unfulfilled, restless and discontented.

To the extent that I am being true to myself, present, in every moment, I am controlling what happens to my person; I am being responsible, and the circumstances of my life will combine to work towards harmony, the right and the good.

There is no fate, accident or chance which can alter my circumstances, only I who must change them by changing myself within. I am the circumstances of my life."

This, the unbearable truth of the law of life, as you will see, leaves you no room for self-delusion or escape — no time.

Time as something that separates us from events in the past or future, is the dream, the unconsciousness, that we escape into to avoid the truth of our lives or ourselves, now. You are either true now or you are not. You cannot be true yesterday or tomorrow.

164

There is no right and wrong. There is only right, which is to be true, now. And there is no one or any thing to be true to — only this moment, this everlasting moment of oneself within which is the true and the truth.

Although all the unconscious people of the earth must remain oblivious to the justice of the karmic law, they cannot escape its overall effect which is the circumstances of the world itself. Here the law, as the condition of the world, works itself out very slowly from one life-sequence, or dream, to another: that which is not faced up to in one sequence — or in any moment — must be faced up to in the next, or the next, or the next, until the truth of the law finally becomes the living truth of oneself, the being — and one awakes.

This is the reality of time and existence.

This is karma.

35
NOTHING FOR NOTHING

The law of life says that no human being is more special than any other: all are equal; or alternatively, all are special and therefore are all still equal.

And yet existence shows us that all are not equal. At every level, the rich, the privileged, the sleek and the healthy enjoy a very special position not available to all.

Where is the truth and justice of the law in this?

The truth, according to the law, is that every person in existence is special because every single one possesses more than some other person somewhere.

The fact that some have more than others for a time is irrelevant. Even she or he who has the least, says the law, still has more than nothing so is still special. To exist is to possess something, even if it is only a body. Less than that is to have nothing — and that is to be dead.

The law of life also says that in existence you get nothing for nothing. Everything has to be paid for. Without exception, everyone must pay. Because no one is special.

And without exception, everyone *is* paying. To be in existence, to live, is to pay. Everyone is paying today in the circumstances of their lives for what they received in the past. And what they are receiving today as other circumstances in their lives, if not already earned, will have to be paid for in the future, in time.

Thus, for everyone who comes and goes on the earth, does the supreme justice work timelessly in time.

All payment due under the law of life is made in time — in time having to be spent in existence. Time is the currency of being in existence, as money is the currency of living in existence.

Whatever is owed must be paid for here on the earth, sooner or later. That payment at any time appears as the difficult circumstances and problems in one's life. And the ultimate payment on earth at any time is made with one's body — death.

When you call on the law of life for justice by facing up to the truth of yourself at any moment, you ask for an immediate accounting. You ask to be shown the balance between what you have received in the matter troubling you and what you have given; or between what you are paying now and what is due. You are not asking to be judged on any other matter; only this one which is your immediate problem now. You can only face up to one problem in any moment and that is always the one causing you the greatest pain or awareness now.

By appealing direct to life through being brave

enough to take conscious, responsible action, you cut out time and enter the present, or the presence of the truth of yourself. And you are given an immediate assessment or reckoning.

This, the balance owing either way, will soon manifest for you to observe for yourself as new circumstances in your life.

There is no greater justice or truth than this. It is self-evident and unerring. It is the mystery, the secret and truth that all philosophies and religions have tried to find or express.

If you are true in what you are doing, the circumstances will be helpful. But if you are not being as true as you could be — which means you are owing — you may get ill, suffer even a mild illness that normally you would not have considered significant; you may lose some money, have a fierce or exhausting emotional argument, or go through a period of severe frustration, depression or uncertainty to do with your work, partner, housing or family.

The improvements or difficulties often appear immediately.

But they may also not surface for days, weeks or even months. The time-lag can be considerable.

Also, for the individual starting to wake up and become more conscious, the delay can be increased by old habitual emotions re-asserting themselves and causing bouts of resentment, anger and sullen resistance to the working of the law.

Usually, there is some catching up to do. After facing up to one problem you find another you've ignored. Each involves a separate accounting until you've faced or accounted for them all.

But the merit is: you are no longer making more problems for yourself as normal unconscious living does; you are reducing them and renewing yourself at the same time.

As you persevere, you will realise more and more that you are actually living under the law as a way of life, or as a way of love, and that its timeless, faultless justice is working in you and for you. Your life is clearer, cleaner. You are more in charge. You could never return to the old way again.

For the massed population of the earth that cannot be responsible for itself as you the individual can, the karmic account runs on and on without a balance ever being able to be struck.

This is the never-never world of living on borrowed time. Its blatant disregard for the justice of who really owes whom and who really owes what, creates the vicious injustice or imbalance that never stops growing between the poor and the rich, the handicapped and the strong, the starving and the sleek, the deprived and the privileged.

So appallingly ill-balanced has it all become that only the end of time itself, which is now approaching, can settle the account.

Even so, even until then it is all impeccably just. It is all a matter of time. All are paying in time or will have to pay in time. None can escape what is due to him or her as none can be denied.

Since there is no one to take responsibility for the world, or because no one is able to take responsibility for such a dreadful mass of injustice, the karmic adjustments are made automatically from one generation to another as the endless alternating pains and gains of existence.

Owing to the enormous time-lag caused by the massed unconsciousness of what is happening, the debts and reimbursements due to any generation fall on other generations yet to be born: and so it is said that the sins of the fathers shall fall upon the sons.

Any immediate justice gained through isolated individuals being responsible or true to themselves, soon disappears into the chaos and confusion of the whole — an entire world, failing to be responsible for itself, its people, its planet.

Nonetheless, even in the chaos, the law dispenses its timeless chaotic justice: what is due lags behind what is paid; justice lags behind injustice; and every person without exception suffers in time.

36
YOU ARE NOW RESPONSIBLE

For the masses there is no freedom from the ignorance of the world and themselves, no liberation. Only the individual can escape.

You are the individual.

In truth, you are the only individual. For only you can know if you are being true in any moment. The essential characteristic of individuality is to know what is true at any time.

Each individual is at a certain evolutionary point of consciousness. Consciousness is awareness of the truth of yourself or of life. Anyone reading this book right through will have developed to a certain stage of consciousness. To a less developed person it will seem meaningless. However, as consciousness or truth cannot really vary or have degrees, when we talk of developing consciousness in people it is more accurate to say that each individual is at a certain evolutionary stage of being less ignorant or less unconscious.

Because you have read this far — because you are real and serious enough to be able to hear the truth of life, your life — you have reached a certain point of consciousness: you are now answerable to the karmic law.

As never before, you now control the circumstances of your life. How conditions unfold and affect you from now on will depend increasingly on how true you are being to yourself. It is a mighty moment and one to be uplifted by.

Whatever your reaction is to what I have just said, you have no choice. You can't run away or opt out. It is already done under the law. Like it or not like it, you are now responsible for yourself. And every time you perceive yourself being irresponsible, you will know it.

The law of life's eternal justice is that no one can come under its conscious control until all the implications and consequences have been explained to them; or until they perceive the truth of it through their own experience.

In other words, no one is responsible under the law for what they do not know. Knowledge is responsibility. And now you know.

Furthermore, you now have the power to help you to be true as never before, even though you may not realise it immediately. This power comes from the energy of your new self-knowledge—your knowledge of the law as I have explained it. You and the law are one, although you may not know that yet either.

Whenever you have the opportunity to be true, or more true to yourself, this energy will rise up in your consciousness to remind you. How swiftly and often you notice the reminder will depend on your diminishing inner resistance to the truth — your reducing independence or forgetfulness of the law.

This independence is deeply ingrained in everyone as the ignorance and unconsciousness of the human race — until the individual is able to rise above it in himself or herself by being true every moment without effort.

From now on, if ever you are not being true to yourself, if you are aware of it and persist in it, you will automatically draw to yourself the circumstances to make you more responsible and true in that area.

Invariably, these are self-corrective or painful.

The justice of the law is such that in time you will actually see yourself creating difficult circumstances in yourself, or perpetuating them.

The main barrier to truth is fear plus the desire to remain physically comfortable and emotionally secure even though these particular conditions are constantly making you unhappy.

Remember, what continues to trouble you is what you are not facing up to — and are in fact running from.

In any situation you can do no more than your best. It is the awareness — the growing consciousness of the need to be true for truth's sake and no other — that counts.

Failure does not matter. You must not dwell on the past. There will be no shortage of opportunities to try again. Life will see to that — as life will also ensure that you succeed more and more; until eventually you perceive the wonder of the law working with precision in your life as you begin to work the miracle of controlling circumstances as yourself.

37
REINCARNATION
IS NOT THE TRUTH

Existence is ignorance or unconsciousness in motion. And the purpose of it is to make the individual man or woman more conscious.

This is done through the karmic process of death and rebirth which, for the masses, is the unending cycle of time or existence. For only through ignorance, or what is false — that is, through the person that you think you are but are not — can the individual being that you really are ever perceive the truth of itself.

In other words, you have to be in ignorance in person in order to emerge from ignorance as your individual conscious self or true being.

But you must be clear as to what death and rebirth is and not mix it up with popular notions that the person or masses have of it today.

For instance, reincarnation as it is discussed and understood in the world, is not the truth. Reincarnation is a doctrinal falsehood, a reasonable attempt to give integrity to the continued existence of ignorance as a way of life.

In other words, reincarnation is the doctrine of ignorance playing for time in the future so that it won't have to face up to being true to life in the present.

The only death and rebirth for you, the individual, is now. This moment is your only incarnation. You can only be incarnate, in the flesh, now, as you can only be true now. You can't be true yesterday or tomorrow. You are always true or not true now.

If you quit a situation or a person in order to be true to yourself, it will be now, not tomorrow.

In that moment and all the other moments of your daily life when you have the opportunity to be true or not true to yourself or life, you either die (to be true) or you do not die (to be true). You either die in that moment to the person that you are — die to the ignorance that you are holding onto or compromising with as yourself — or you don't.

If you die to that personal self — which means you face up to the falsehood of it — you are immediately reborn, instantly freed of that part of the old person or false self that you were. If you don't die to it, you continue to live on as the same old person, the same old wearying problem you can't escape from.

The person is the only problem.

Getting the person to the point of dying, however, is unpleasant, uncomfortable, difficult or painful, as everyone knows who has had to be brave and true and face up to themselves in a crisis. But the release, the blessed cleansing energy that comes from being straight and new is unmistakable.

Only fear, the fear of dying now to what you are used to, stands in the way. Only fear dies.

38
THE PROCESS OF DYING

The process of dying and rebirth is the same, whether you die psychologically, emotionally or physically.

Something dies within you. It is you but it is not you. Your attention is focussed on that within. You feel the dying. You don't see it, imagine it or think about it. It is intensely though very finely agitating — disturbing, distressing, painful, not unlike the after-effects of a wasp or bee sting, or the high-pitched onset of a dose of 'flu. You watch without seeing, acutely aware as you endeavour to perceive — through the confusion of psychological death, through the pain of emotional death, or through the incredible palpable blackness of physical death.

At the moment of dying, the physical body which at all other times seems so unquestionably you, together with all notions about reincarnation or any other topic, is completely irrelevant to you, has no reality at all.

Death is death. There is nothing like it. Even though you die ten thousand times — which developing consciousness or evaporating ignorance must — you can't remember death. If you do, you only think you do and what you remember is still a part of a living, of holding on notionally — not death itself.

In death you grow in being, not in information.

Death is always the first time. Each death is new, for death is now.

Ignorance lives in the past and fears the now, the present which is death to it. Unless you die continuously to your notional self while you are living, you will always fear death as it approaches. You will hold on. And you will be distressed, disturbed or pained in your unhappiness.

Death exists only for the living, the living ignorance that must die. When the ignorance dies, life is — and you feel and know you are reborn.

Remember, death in all its facets is the process of being made true by being made to face up to the parts of yourself that you have conveniently ignored or excused in the past.

Remember, death always takes place *inside* the physical body, within, where there is no physical body — only feeling, sensation or presence — and no thought.

In that brief moment, even though you may still be living in the body, you are out of existence; you have overcome the world and are out of time.

In that brief moment all your debts are paid.

39

THE REPETITION OF IGNORANCE

For reincarnation to have any meaning there has to be a knowing self that continues from one life-on-earth through death to another life-on-earth.

No such self exists.

You, the person who assumes a past and future with all its problems, memories, fears, ambitions, likes and dislikes, wants and ideals, die with the body and are never seen or heard of again.

Nevertheless, your awareness and presence (they are one and the same) survives physical death.

But that presence is never born again into another body.

Only the body and its ignorance of that immortal reality of your self is born. And that is not a return but a repetition, a gradual re-arising of the same ignorance which continues and will continue as long as I mistake or identify with the body as my self.

When I who am the awareness, the consciousness in the body, am no longer ignorant of my true self, the re-embodiment of my ignorance ceases. I realise that as my being is pure awareness there is nothing to reincarnate, nothing to be born and nothing to die.

Ignorance begins with the notion, "I am the body".

It commences the moment my body is conceived in the womb.

But the ignorance only starts to become personal — or painful — after my body is born and I perceive other bodies or objects to be separate from it, separate from what I now regard as myself.

Then through infancy my ignorance slowly develops into a knowledgeable person, I, who derive all my values, knowledge and unhappiness from the erroneous identification with the body.

Would you please test this for yourself?

What is your problem, your deepest worry?

It derives from your identification with the body, your person. Hence the person, because it has no awareness of its true self or presence which is beyond problems and death, is ignorance personified. The person is the cause of all suffering.

Yet the person, like all its problems and frustrations, is completely false, as unreal as the notion of the feathers of an elephant. Just as there can be no feathers of an elephant apart from the frustrating notion of such a thing, there is no person, apart from the person's frustrating notion of himself or herself. The person is the illusion, the surmise, that grows out of the elephant, the body.

Since the person is unreal, whatever the person conceives is as unreal and inevitably troublesome as itself.

Consequently, everything personal in existence, being unreal, perishes. That includes the body out of which the bogus person arose in the first place and without which the person and all its problems simply vanishes.

To make all this clearer, I am going to show you in your own experience how ignorance is conceived. I am going to take you back into the womb where it all started, where the body itself arises. For this, we won't need a psychiatrist, a hypnotist or any other kind of expert. We need only the truth — and your impersonal awareness. Anything additional will be purely the delusion of the person.

We will proceed very slowly. As we do, see if you recognise the truth of what I am saying. For it is the truth of yourself. Come with me step by step. Examine every word in your own experience at that moment. Don't analyse. Just relax, read and be.

And after you've read what I'm going to say, read it over and over again until you start to perceive the wonder of what it all means. This will happen naturally without any effort or trying, as long as you keep reading. For what you begin to perceive or reunite with will be your true self, the eternal awareness and presence that is always there when the person, the striving, doubting problem-maker, is not.

40
LIFE, BEFORE CONCEPTION

Ⅰt is undeniable, is it not, that you are life?

And is it not true that the life you are now — not the person or the body — is already in the womb before conception and at conception?

In other words, life in every instance before conception is in the womb. Without life, the womb cannot conceive.

Life is always present before any form of life appears.

Even today you frequently have this experience of life-before-the-body. But the mind, the ignorant person, glosses over it. And so it's lost. Let me show you.

Life, with its extraordinary quality of pure awareness, is often experienced as you are waking up from sleep in the morning — before you come to realise you've got a body and start associating with the problems of the day. What is that awareness which is indisputably you before your body consciousness, your problems, come to mind?

It is life — you, which is always present before any form of life, any body including your own body appears. The awareness, the life in you, is there first, fully aware. If you think you haven't had this experience, you now will before long. When it happens just be very still and observe without thinking.

Let me give you another example of yourself as pure life or awareness. This occurs when you wake up with a start out of a sound sleep and for a split second don't know where you are or who you are; yet you are acutely aware of being aware, extremely alert and present. There is no knowledge of any body or any thing. Who or what is that awareness — that pure consciousness which is without knowledge or knowing before experience rushes in?

It is life, you, before the body, before conception.

★

Where there is no life there is no awareness, no waking up, no experience — and no conception. And where there is no conception there is no body. You, life, are first, before conception, before the body and before the idea of the body's form; in short, before you come to your senses.

This life, this awareness and presence which you are now behind the concept of your body, is your being. Or more simply, life is being behind the body.

Without realising it, you spend half your life in the fullness and completeness of this state — in dreamless sleep. Dreamless sleep — when you are your true self without any body or person — is the most consistently perfect thing in your life. Each day you seek it and look forward to it with unfailing relish.

The reason you think that in dreamless sleep you are not aware and fulfillingly conscious, is because in the moment you think about it you're already awake and identified with the body and the person.

The body and the person have no direct knowledge of life itself. They are external to life. They know only forms of life — life perceived through the senses — and forms of life are not life. Life is always within.

In dreamless sleep where your awareness is one with life, one with your true being, all forms have disappeared including your body and your person.

Yet when you awake you still know you slept soundly. How do you know you slept soundly if there is no awareness of being in that state?

The answer, of course, is that you *do* know — don't you? It is knowledge without form — pure knowledge, *self-knowledge*. If anyone tried to deny that you slept soundly they would never convince you — because you know it as yourself. You are aware of being, even though you can't remember it!

It's amazing, isn't it, when you look at it? By saying you slept soundly you acknowledge having had continuous awareness of undisturbed, unconditioned being, or life. You acknowledge an indescribable continuity of the being of yourself which in your waking condition you can still actually appreciate as something non-existent yet undeniably positive and desirable — real.

Deep dreamless sleep is simply the total negation

and disappearance of your false identification with the body and the person. You then recover or return to your natural awareness of the presence of life, your true self or being, as you were before conception in the womb.

To bring that state of dreamless sleep or pre-conception into your awareness while you are alive and awake is the ultimate self-knowledge — self realisation.

41
CONCEPTION AND BIRTH

The word conception, or to conceive, as you probably have noticed, has two apparently different meanings. One is to receive or be pregnant with a baby or embryo physical body; the other is to receive or be pregnant with an idea or notion.

By you and I now looking at the conception of the body in the womb, we can see for ourselves how the two meanings — the physical and the abstract — actually describe what happens at the instant of conception.

The body is the initial object through which life comes into existence. This occurs at the moment of conception in the womb.

The question is, who or what conceives the body? The womb obviously doesn't conceive; conception merely occurs in the womb.

So who or what conceives the body?

Life does.

You, life, the being behind the womb, conceive

your own body and your own existence.

This is the secret behind life on earth and the source of all reincarnation theories. To understand the whole astonishing process it is necessary to go back even beyond the womb, beyond dreamless sleep into life after physical death — and this I do later. Meanwhile, we will continue observing life coming into existence into the womb.

I was saying that you, life, the being of pure awareness behind the womb, conceive your own existence.

You do this in the womb or through the womb where all life originates by identifying with the first potentially complete human form — meaning a fertilised egg — that enters your awareness. This you receive, conceive and give life to by identifying with it and perceiving through its incipient senses of feeling.

The effect is much the same as today when you can look at a totally lifeless photograph of someone you love and by identifying with the photo, experience your love of the person through it, although clearly the image has no life outside yourself, outside of what you are giving it.

So in the womb you provide the embryo with your beingness by conceiving it as the feeling of yourself; and at the same time you give it life and identity by conceiving it as I, your notion of yourself as that feeling.

This is the fundamental error of human existence. From this all error, all ignorance arises. The body you have assumed in the womb, and the equally false notion that I-am-this-body, are now gestating, that is, swelling and growing as forms of life, forms of yourself, which are not yourself.

Fertilisation — the bond or union of male and female matter — is the magnet that draws unlimited life and being into limited individual existence.

Whereas previously your awareness was endless, undisturbed being or bliss without object or subject, there is now the body object, and I the subject.

Existence has begun for you. From now on that form and its existence are "your life".

★

After conception, the first sense of awareness I the embryo have is of the utter warmth, comfort and congeniality of the womb.

Nearing the end of nine months I am addicted to this perfection, this seemingly complete, self-sustaining feeling existence. I — my feeling body — and my world — the womb — are in almost total harmony. Body and world are one.

At birth, as I am pushed out of my mother's body, this unity is violently shattered. The warmth, comfort and effortless peace of the womb vanish.

I am plunged into cold space and discomfort. The change is profoundly disturbing. It produces an awareness of insecurity, unrelatedness or the first feelings of confusion, self-doubt.

There is the immediate sense of duality. There is I the body and that which is not my body — the impinging hostile surrounding conditions. For the first time I am conscious of lack — lack of the perfection of the warmth and comfort inseparable from myself.

I am woeful. I know longing. And gradually I know pain.

I want what I had, the past, what I was and felt in the womb — my original perception of myself as the sense of warmth, comfort and peace.

I am frustrated. I now know the feeling of frustration. I want something other than what I have or am — and can do nothing about it. I am helpless, isolated, bewilderingly alone — incredibly lonely.

My body cries. It cries for warmth and comfort — the succour, security and enfolding presence of the moist and gentle womb. But this has gone forever.

From this moment on for the rest of my life I will identify with, or name as love, any conditions able to reproduce in me feelings or impressions similar to those I knew in the womb. I will love anything or anyone whose presence arouses these responses in me. And my whole life will be a constant endeavour to acquire and hold on to those things and people.

But in this I will always fail or be disappointed. For the only way I can have the love and union I crave is by returning or re-entering the physical womb. This I will later attempt to do through the brief palliative of physical sex. I will then identify sex with love — and make yet another error.

I will identify love with any condition, person or thing that provides even a degree of that sense of original warmth, peace or comfort of the womb which I can never hope to find again outside myself.

After leaving the womb, my first real awareness of love is my mother. (Oh doctors and nurses delivering me to her, please embrace my body firmly with your warm skin, secure arms and good will). My mother's nipple in my mouth, the warmth and succour of her milk flowing into my body and the warmth and smell of her flesh outside me, provide a sense of reassurance, an incipient feeling of love, of some sort of return to what I had known.

So through my strange new senses I begin to project myself further out from my body — attaching to her through smell, touch-feeling and taste as transient substitutes for the contentment I knew.

But could anything ever replace the effortless warmth, comfort and security of the womb where there was no need of any object apart from myself? No. Only death perhaps — which in my greatest misery, as I grow older in the body, I will sometimes wish for.

My new-found love or identity with my mother's body, my sense of being and belonging, is continually interrupted. I cry. I learn how to cry and when to cry to try to bring some love into this weird, alien existence — until even crying becomes a kind of perverse comfort against the sense of loss and pain. I cry not so much out of discomfort, but for what I feel I have lost. It will always be like that from now on.

So I will live this life crying and trying to bring about the impossible — to materialise that which I left in the womb. As this is impossible while I think I am the body, I will never be happy or contented for long until I die.

Such is the fate of ignorance.

Section Three
part two

DYING TO BE BORN

Death and the Secret of Hell

42
AFTER DEATH

Why does it all happen in the first place?

What is the reason for existence, the cause of it? How do I, life or awareness, come to be in the womb? How is it that I, who am unlimited life or consciousness, take up such a limited position, or any position at all?

The answer lies in death, behind the death of the physical body.

With the body dies the person — your fears, doubts, hopes, memories, ambitions, likes and dislikes, wants and ideals. They were all substitutes, anyway, for the knowledge that there is no death; and when you die and discover this they vanish as the ignorance they were.

In death you lose nothing but your ignorance. Ignorance is mortal. Death is the loss of that mortality.

So in death only your presence and awareness-without-knowledge-or-ignorance survive.

Your experience of this awareness, this pure life that you are, I have demonstrated in the examples of dreamless sleep and waking from sleep. Now I will explain what your presence is.

While you are alive, your presence is almost totally insulated or obscured from your own and other people's experience of it by your body.

The living body is a continuously mummifying outer vestige, being left behind moment-to-moment as the past by your more swiftly vibrating, more timeless presence, within. In short, the body is the living record in sense — the stuff of space and time — of your fleeting presence on earth. This record it registers as ageing and finally as death.

However, physical space and time are a very small part of your existence.

At death, when your consciousness is relieved of the body insulation, you are aware of your presence, your immortality, for the first time. The feeling of liberation is ecstatic.

Persons close to you whom you leave behind may also register your presence at this time. Those who do will have no doubt, even though your dead body is lying in front of them or already disposed of, that the unseen presence is you, the unmistakable living you.

This presence *is* you — whereas your body is never you because it lags too far behind you, behind the immediacy of your bodiless presence.

What does this presence consist of ?

At death, it is the sum total of your life just concluded. That life has not ended. It is really just beginning. At the moment of death you are filled with life, abundant with the energetic presence of the life just lived. You are like a bee returning to the hive from the orchard of the earth, pollen sacks laden with living life.

Living is actually gathering. You have gathered, stored and brought with you every energetic instant of that life. You *are* that life. That life is your presence or self.

So in death, as in your mother's womb before conception, you are still life. However that life which then was awareness alone, now has presence in it — the presence of the self you have gathered.

You are conscious as never before. But you have no perceived body. You are a point of consciousness from which you observe the earthly scene. Gradually that earthly perception fades.

You then pass through hell.

Hell is an energy that purges you of the residual "hell" in yourself, your negative emotions — such as hate — and especially appetites that went deeper than those normally attached to the physical consciousness and left behind with your physical body.

Any pain or "hell" you suffer is only of your own making: what you liked too much or disliked too much and lost yourself in. Hell merely provides the reflection for you to perceive the attachment in yourself. The perceiving of it is the dissolution or "burning out" of this negative worldliness still clinging to you.

Hell is an essential part of death, a purification process before you go on. Everyone must pass through it but not everyone suffers.

You then begin the work of life after death.

That work is to extract from your presence the true value of the life just lived. You do this by literally consuming yourself, dissolving yourself. You relive that life. You relive it, not in the shallow, lateral A-to-B way as it was lived by the old mortal body/mind, but as your new, hypersensitive, immortal consciousness.

You live it with a wondrous intensity and fullness. From every living moment of that life's seeming pain, pleasure, love and indifference, you extract the true meaning, significance and purpose — which was impossible in your former condition of ignorance on earth, and innate selfishness that hell removed. You become totally absorbed in your new life and are continuously amazed by it.

Three outstanding things are being done in the process.

First, you are extracting the affirmative value of your life, distilling the whole experience into a minute divine essence or fragrance of yourself. This is eternal or real consciousness, as distinct from immortal consciousness. You are reaping all the moments in which you were true.

Second, in a contrary, negative sense you are registering in your awareness what you now clearly see was missing from your earth life to give it more reality; that is, you are noting earthly experiences which in your immortal wisdom you perceive would eliminate some of your ignorance and make you more true, more real, if there was to be another chance.

Third, the residue of your former self or life left by this continuous purifying process is forming your new immortal psychic body and life.

This psychic body of consciousness, which you now are in life-after-death, although immortal, is not eternal.

The order of existence is from the physical to the immortal to the eternal — the three worlds. In the after-death process you contribute simultaneously to each world. That is, while you are extracting your eternal essence that "goes to" the eternal world, you are forming the negative impression that will determine your next physical life; and at the same time you are automatically creating your immortal body and through it living your immortal life.

You are not gathering experience as you did on earth. You are actually shedding all your experience, your past, by transforming and transmuting it into relative forms of the present. In becoming less, you are becoming more — more real.

At death, if your consciousness is not yet sufficiently evolved to sustain a conscious presence — that is, if your eternal self or divine essence has not been sufficiently realised through living on earth — you will die unconscious.

You will still create an immortal body but it will be a vaguer sort of dream body, something like you used to create in sleep on earth to release your anxieties and frustrations. Your life after death will then be a subjective dream: wonderful, but still a dream. You will be unable to step out of your own past presence, out of your own limited life or dream, into the greater presence or world of life-beyond-death.

Life-beyond-death is the next phase following life-after-death.

The world of life-beyond-death is an objective world, that is, a world real in its own right, which is unimaginable. But to participate in it you have to have a real body, a fully responsible body. That body is the golden dream-body and has to be made by you through your conscious presence and conscious love on earth.

43
THE DREAM-BODIES

The whole scheme of existence depends on what is done on earth. Only on earth is freedom from ignorance attained.

You must understand that all existence before death and after death is a dream. It is an increasingly real dream, but still a dream. Hence the need of a dream-body.

A dream-body cannot last indefinitely. The lowest dream-body of the three worlds of existence is the physical body and it dissolves or dies very quickly. The immortal or psychic body of life-after-death is far more enduring. But finally, after you have dissolved yourself, used up the force of the psychic self or presence behind it, it too disintegrates and vanishes.

The golden dream-body is the realest body in existence. It is the body of life-beyond-death which is the state above life-after-death.

Everyone has formed or realised a degree of this

body which is their own true self, their divinity as consciousness, the reality they are endeavouring through existence to be. It is the body or realm of the great spirits who provide, or are, the order of existence. It is eternal. It is eternity itself. It is one with God's will, God's presence but is still beneath God.

The inferior immortal or psychic dream-body of life-after-death has an enormous range of possibilities of existence for the individual, depending on his or her state of consciousness. Like a gradient, the psychic body or psychic life extends from the basest, densest emotions, more destructive than anything encountered in the physical, to the highest, finest and most splendid examples of selfless divine love.

As fragrance or divine essence — which can be likened to a combination of smell, taste and sweetness or feeling — represents the eternal, so colour-tones represent the immortal.

At its lowest, the immortal psychic body is a dirty, dark brown or red. The middle range is from red to rose. The highest is yellow to gold. Gold is yellow with divine presence in it — hence the golden body.

As a consciousness ascends the psychic gradient, it becomes more real, more timeless, more indefinable until finally it disappears forever into the eternal nothing, the pre-existent all that is God.

No one on earth is the highest colour all the time. Man and woman in the physical are a constantly changing flux of colour-tones from the highest, through the intermediate, to the low—responding every moment to the waves of time or past that flow through the body from the human subconscious.

Life expectancy in the immortal world can be ten

times longer than is normal on earth. Time is slower or more profound because consciousness is swifter and needs less time. But the immortal body can only live or be sustained as long as any trace of the previous earth life or old presence remains to be transformed. Immediately this raw material is exhausted the immortal life is over and the immortal body vanishes.

You are then, once more, awareness or life alone. Time has virtually ceased. You have no presence because you have used it all up — therefore no personal life to reflect off. There is nothing for your immortal consciousness to perceive.

At any time you can only perceive what you are. Had existence on earth allowed you to produce enough essence, higher golden consciousness, you would be perceiving that resplendent eternal world and be eternal.

But as it is for most people, all you are, and all you had in the combined existence of before and after death, you have dissolved or transmuted. And there was not enough reality in it. But there is no need to be anxious because your essence from each life — your individual eternal consciousness — "ascends" and remains in the eternal world. It is this you are holding on to, reflecting off, when you are under the pressure of being true while alive.

By the time you are able to read this book and take responsibility for your life, you can be assured you have established a reachable divine presence or consciousness in the eternal world.

Although each life-contribution is minute, in death — whether physical death, or emotional death in the moment of being true — you are being compelled to build yourself, make yourself, give yourself a more real reflection amidst the ignorance that is every life on earth.

44
THE ANTE-ROOM
OF EXISTENCE

So now, after the death of your immortal body, you have no presence at all. No one on either side of existence could recognise you.

Neither can you come back into either world in any real sense of returning or reincarnating because you are nothing — nothing but indistinguishable awareness, life. This awareness or life that you now are is universal — the same indistinguishable and unknowable awareness that is in everyone. So there is nothing meaningful to return.

Even if you did re-enter existence on earth — reincarnate — you would not remember yourself because you have no self. What you might then think you remember as yourself, as your previous life which some people do, would be only the memory of your past ignorance.

Such memories are meaningless because ignorance has no meaning in life — only in living, where all it excites is more ignorance. In existence, all you can ever remember is what you are not.

Yet in your particular nothingness after the death of your immortal body, you are not complete. Your nothingness has a negative or wishful value. It contains the negative impression you registered earlier — that minus imprint of something imagined to be missing as experience from your previous presence or life on earth.

In other words, your awareness is not pure nothing. You are zero minus one, nothing minus something. You are a negative potential, a wish, a dream, a tale, a fantasy that has not yet been. You are life or awareness with a distinctive, negative stamp, in other words a uniquely incomplete character. You are ignorance of life ready to exist again.

This is you as pure ego. Pure ego — purified of self — is only possible in the state before conception.

Irresistibly, your negative pure egoic awareness is drawn into the univeral womb or chamber of existence.

This is an extraordinary place. It is the ante-room of physical existence. Every human womb on earth leads here.

Here, all life that has completed the death process waits to come into existence, to enter the purely human illusion that there is some sort of fulfilment, completion or perfection to be gained in time—a notion which has no reality whatever except in mankind's negative potential, his ignorance or imagination.

Here in this amazing place you wait, knowing and feeling nothing other than a subtle energetic anticipation or excitation which arises from your incompleteness.

And you know nothing of what is being described here because that is from the overview of the eternal consciousness, the golden body.

Your egoic awareness is perceiving absolutely nothing. It is in an untroubled limbo. If you could know anything, which you cannot, you would know only what you are lacking, that is, what you are unconsciously waiting for. And what that is you are about to find out — by conceiving it in the flesh as your new earth-life, and then living it.

Further, you cannot recognise or know where you are, what this womb or chamber of all existence is. So you do not know that it is hell.

You are in hell.

But you are not suffering because there is nothing left in you to burn. You have no self. Only self suffers or burns in hell.

In former times, this utterly incomprehensible energy or hell of human pain, when glimpsed from the earth side, was likened to an eternal fire, a flaming furnace or a boiling cauldron — all due to man's limited concepts to describe destructive intensity. In the imagery of our modern world, the hellish nature of this energy is comparable to the first instant at the centre of an atomic explosion, or the destructively creative process inside a star.

Hell is the powerhouse of existence.

To exist on earth all life has to come out through hell. And at death all life must pass back through hell. Death is the process of "coming out" reversed. The energy of hell itself is constant and unvarying. But the effect on life coming and going is radically different.

45
THE SECRET OF HELL

On earth, the energy of hell is sex.
Sex is hell.

To all human life coming into existence through hell, hell is craving.

So sex or hell on earth is also craving.

To the incoming life, the craving of hell is for experience, physical existence.

No experience — no existence — is possible without sex, without hell, as all human beings come into existence through sex or hell.

So sex is the key to the mystery of life and hell on earth.

Your negative awareness, now waiting in hell before existence, seethes with hellish intensity for the sensuous experience you need.

You are sexual craving itself. Together with all the other human life waiting for existence in the universal womb, you represent the one sexual desire or craving experienced by every man and woman on earth.

You are no longer pure ego. You are lust — the lust for life in the flesh.

You are now the ultimate in selfish egoic desire to have what you want — your own physical experience.

The intensity of your craving draws the earthly couples together, forces them to mate. You are their unquenchable thirst for union. You — the disembodied — draw the embodied back to the womb through the vagina, back towards hell, where you wait.

None can resist your fascination — in thought, feeling or action. You are unbridled sex, the insatiable, inexplicable appetite that brings shame, guilt, pain, horror and despair into the world. None escapes you. You consider no-one and nothing, neither the good, the innocent, nor the young.

Fiendish, devilish is your one-pointed egoic drive that day and night, sucks a river of eggs from the human bodies of the earth in coupling and masturbation. Endlessly the river flows on but without waste, for life exists only to provide you with your endless stream of bodies. To you, life's purpose is the embodied ecstasy of life giving life to itself, in the flesh without restraint. You are the power that makes life on earth possible.

Sooner or later your egoic negativity, seething for life in the womb, perceives a positivity. This is the moment when in a particular womb the male sperm and female egg unite and bond. It occurs when both the actual and potential conditions on the earth — the positive polarity — matches sufficiently the negative polarity, the circumstances you need for your life on earth.

With hellish negative intensity or craving, you

fix on this positive physical bond in the womb and conceive it as yourself.

Onto the embryo's comparatively weak, fleshy or mortal positivity, you impress your enormous, irresistible, psychic or immortal negativity.

The positive flesh of the embryo becomes negative — filled with desire — a negative of yourself, of your own fantastic craving. You have physically impregnated the embryo with your missing life, your missing self — your life to be.

From now on the embryo's overwhelming negative, psychic or egoic polarity will attract to itself the positive earthly circumstances you crave.

You have cloned yourself.

Frequently, the weak mortal bond of the embryo cannot stand the massive force or charge of your psychic negativity — and miscarriage occurs.

46
LIBERATION

You are the eternal contradiction.

Since, before conception, you are the sexual craving of immortal life itself, you are the paradox of life craving for life and death at the same time: immortality craving for a fleshly form of life that will inevitably die.

As sex, you give the greatest pleasure and the greatest pain; as the hell of death, the greatest grief and the greatest release. Through sexual union you crave for the extinction of your own craving by sacrificing your immortal awareness to mortal existence — so that you may crave and live again to die and crave again.

You are endless life, endless living and dying, endless pain and pleasure, endless past, endless karma.

You are the egoic player of the immortal game played in flesh, forgetfulness and death — and in the partial awakening after death to another existence which reveals nothing but what you have already been.

You are immortal. But you are not eternal. You are not uncontained, unlimited life. You are not the purity of hell itself.

You are just used by hell, put through hell without ever knowing what the hell is really happening. By your craving you are bound forever to the illusory cycle of life-and-death existence — until the incomprehensible truth of it shines through in the reflection of your own eternal consciousness.

When this happens you are eternal. You then see through the ego that you were. At the same time you see through hell, and no longer go through it or are touched by it again.

For hell in reality is none other than the eternal flame. And the eternal flame is none other than the eternal body of the eternal spirit.

The apparent devilish intensity that never lets you rest is its eternal love.

Through death and craving, through one and then the other, the eternal draws you ever towards itself — uncontained, unconditioned eternal life, liberation from all ignorance, all existence.

*For information about Barry Long's work
and details of his other publications
write to*

*The Barry Long Foundation
BCM Box 876, London WC1N 3XX
England*

———————

*The Barry Long Centre (Australia)
PO Box 1260, Southport, Qld 4215
Australia*